passing
numerical
reasoning
tests

passing numerical reasoning tests

Rob Williams

PEARSON

Harlow, England • London • New York • Boston • San Francisco • Toronto • Sydney
Auckland • Singapore • Hong Kong • Tokyo • Seoul • Taipei • New Delhi
Cape Town • São Paulo • Mexico City • Madrid • Amsterdam • Munich • Paris • Milan

PEARSON EDUCATION LIMITED

Edinburgh Gate
Harlow CM20 2JE
United Kingdom
Tel: +44 (0)1279 623623
Web: www.pearson.com/uk

First edition published 2015 (print and electronic)

Pearson Education is not responsible for the content of third-party internet
sites.

ISBN: 978–1–292–01541–5 (print)
       978–1–292–01543–9 (PDF)
       978–1–292–01544–6 (ePub)
       978–1–292–01542–2 (eText)

British Library Cataloguing-in-Publication Data
A catalogue record for the print edition is available from the British Library

Library of Congress Cataloging-in-Publication Data
A catalog record for the print edition is available from the Library of Congress

10 9 8 7 6 5 4 3 2 1
18 17 16 15 14

Print edition typeset in 10/14pt by 3
Printed in Malaysia (CTP-PPSB)

NOTE THAT ANY PAGE CROSS REFERENCES REFER TO THE PRINT
EDITION

Contents

About the author   vi
Acknowledgements   vii
Foreword   viii

part 1 Getting to grips with your test   1

   1 Getting started   5

   2 Practice makes perfect   13

   3 Brush up your maths skills   23

   4 Succeed on test day   37

part 2 Time to practise   49

   5 Basic numerical reasoning tests   53

   6 Numerical comprehension tests   69

   7 Warm-up numerical reasoning tests   89

   8 Numerical critical reasoning tests   133

   9 Numerical data interpretation tests   155

  10 Advanced numerical data interpretation   183

About the author

Rob Williams is a chartered occupational psychologist with over twenty years' experience in the design and delivery of ability tests. Having worked for several of the UK's leading test publishers, he has written many numerical reasoning tests and presented his research at home and abroad. His company, Rob Williams Assessment Ltd have designed dozens of ability and personality tests, as well as situational judgment tests (SJTs). Rob specialises in leading test development projects which over the last few years have included tests for European Union employees, for the military and for one of the biggest banks in the United States. When he's not working, Rob enjoys spending time with his two young daughters, going to the cinema and playing tennis.

To find out more, see www.robwilliamsassessment.co.uk.

Acknowledgements

I would like to thank Anne Marie Ryan for her input and advice.

While every effort has been taken to ensure that the practice questions in this book accurately replicate the actual tests, test formats do change periodically. It is therefore wise to always consult your testing organisation's website for the most up-to-date information about your test.

Foreword

Numerical reasoning tests are amongst the most widespread measures that employers apply in selecting staff. I have come across their use for shop-floor factory and retail staff, for computer programmers, croupiers, sales people, managers, space scientists and top civil servants. The last group included the head of the Inland Revenue – the most senior tax job in the United Kingdom – and it was interesting that even there not all of the highly qualified candidates did well! So, numerical reasoning tests are widely valued by employers to help them make distinctions amongst candidates who might otherwise seem to be much of a muchness. I have also become aware that facing a numerical reasoning test is a big challenge for many. It is more often with this type of test than any other that the 'rabbit in the headlights' reaction is found; some people are just too alarmed to demonstrate their true numerical ability. And then there are those who have a blind spot in one or more areas of working with numbers, perhaps going back many years, so that decimals or percentages, say, always floor them.

This book is for all those who can anticipate taking numerical reasoning tests, but who know that they might not do themselves justice – and that is a very large group. It is not only the fearful or those with the blind spots, but also those who are rusty with numbers, perhaps not having had to use them much in their work for several years. The emphasis of the book is on practice, and it is a particularly rich source of sample material of all types of numerical reasoning items that gives readers the opportunity for a dedicated course of exercises to improve their performance. In addition to the sample tests there are a host of tips to ensure that the right approach to practice is adopted, such as examining what might lead you to have guessed an answer and how each bit of practice can be seen as like a single coin – 'not worth much on its own, but valuable when you amass several, giving you a wealth of knowledge'.

Whilst stressing the use of the practice material as such, the book also advises on how to make use of day-to-day opportunities to hone numerical skills. Altogether, this is a very comprehensive and rounded volume for anyone seriously wishing to do brilliantly at numerical reasoning tests.

Dr Robert Edenborough
Director, Bradenlaw Ltd

PART 1

Getting to grips with your test

Every Saturday morning I help my two daughters with their numeracy homework. My younger daughter is still learning her basic mathematical operations and delights in adding up her pocket money. My elder daughter has moved on to fractions and decimals and, if there's a packet of sweets to be shared, is quick to calculate everyone's share. These are numeracy skills that they will be using for the rest of their lives and they are also the very skills you need in order to pass the lowest level 'basic skills' numerical reasoning test.

Although the term 'numerical reasoning' might sound daunting, you don't need to be a mathematical genius in order to pass a test. But you *do* need to be able to accurately perform the numerical operations you learned in school under strictly timed conditions. Nobody is going to tell you off for not doing your homework but preparing for your numerical reasoning test is essential if passing determines the next step in your career or education.

Whether you are an experienced test-taker who uses numerical reasoning skills daily or a beginner who can't remember how to do long division, you will benefit from preparing for your numerical reasoning test. While you might be tempted to jump ahead to Part 2 and start taking practice tests straight away I'd urge you to read Part 1 first. In addition to explaining what numerical reasoning tests are and how they are used, Part 1 aims to help you in three main ways:

1   *Getting the most out of your practice sessions*
    If you have limited time before taking your test it's
    important to use your practice sessions wisely. In Chapter 2
    you will learn how to structure your time and how to ensure
    that you make continual improvements.

2   *Advancing your numerical analysis skills*
    In Chapter 3 you can refresh your numeracy skills and
    discover which mathematical operations are commonly
    used in numerical reasoning tests. There are also helpful
    short cuts and mental maths tips to help you work more
    efficiently.

3   *Improving your test-taking techniques*
    While there's no substitute for actually knowing how to
    calculate the correct answer there are many techniques
    that you can use to boost your test performance. Chapter 4
    features useful test-taking strategies and tactics.

CHAPTER 1

Getting started

When was the last time you did maths at school? Let me guess – was it your least favourite subject? Does the thought of taking a numerical reasoning test strike fear into your heart? If so, don't worry – many people share your anxiety. But remember: anyone can improve with practice!

As a psychometrician I have written many different types of numerical reasoning test. This has given me insights into the strange world of test design, so throughout the first part of this book you will find brilliant test-taking tactics and tips that really work. The second part of this book is packed with practice tests. But first, let's have a look at what numerical reasoning tests are and how they are used.

What is a numerical reasoning test?

A numerical reasoning test is a type of ability test, sometimes referred to as a psychometric or aptitude test. It is designed to measure specific numerical abilities relevant for success in a particular course, profession or job. Numerical reasoning tests are an objective and accurate means of assessing a candidate's potential effectiveness whenever there is a numerical component to a particular job role or course.

What do numerical reasoning tests measure?

a numerical reasoning test is a means of assessing a person's ability to work with numerical information

In simple terms a numerical reasoning test is a means of assessing a person's ability to work with numerical information. These tests provide an objective measure of many numerical reasoning abilities, including the following:

- interpreting statistical data;
- analysing complex mathematical information presented in graphs, pie-charts, tables, etc.;
- solving problems that require an understanding of basic mathematical operations (e.g. fractions, ratios, percentages);
- using and interpreting financial information correctly.

Why do I need to take a numerical reasoning test?

Numerical ability links to job performance, which is why numerical reasoning tests are now used as part of the selection criteria for certain professions and postgraduate degree courses in which it is essential to work effectively with numerical information. Moreover, many medium-sized and large employers make extensive use of ability tests – such as numerical reasoning tests – as part of their standard recruitment and promotion processes. The overall aim is for the best people to be selected, and the use of ability tests differentiates the high performers from the low performers. A well-designed numerical reasoning test is a reliable and consistent means of assessing the skills required for effective performance in that working environment. Ability tests allow employers and university

many medium-sized and large employers make extensive use of ability tests

admissions offices to assess a large number of applicants for competitive positions in a standardised way. The same ability test can be given to a large number of applicants and the results used as an efficient means of comparison. This standardisation makes the process much fairer than relying upon old-fashioned, unstructured interviews where every applicant is asked different questions. Even if you don't like the idea of being tested on your numeracy skills, at least you know that it is fair since everyone has to do the same test!

But I don't want to be a mathematician!

It is not just mathematicians – or even bankers – who need proficient numeracy skills. Everyone uses numeracy skills in daily life – from checking their change in a shop to calculating how long a journey will

> many different jobs require an ability to work confidently with numbers

take. Many different jobs require an ability to work confidently with numbers in order to carry out a range of responsibilities effectively. This could involve anything from interpreting production quotas to carrying out technical work that relies upon detailed calculations. Whereas an accountant will have demonstrated his or her numerical abilities in the process of acquiring a professional qualification, other career paths depend on numerical reasoning tests to measure applicants' skill in this area.

Still not convinced? Let's look at a few jobs that involve more numeracy than you might expect.

Retail sales

Selling isn't just about slick presentation skills and a flair for customer relations. At the entry level, retail sales jobs require the ability to handle money correctly and to deal with customers' transactions competently. Mistakes here could be very costly. At a more senior level, numeracy is used to analyse sales figures, produce account sheets and balance budgets.

Teacher

To teach maths, it makes sense that you would need to be proficient yourself. But many other academic subjects also require dexterity with numbers. For example, all of the sciences use mathematical calculations. Music, design, ICT: all of these fields involve an element of numeracy. Even home economics involves working with measurements. Teachers also need numerical abilities to calculate students' grades, to understand performance targets and to comply with school and departmental budgets.

Manager

Managers need to be able to quickly and effectively digest figures and statistics for their team, department or region. They need to analyse profit and loss figures and to track their own budgets as part of this financial management process. Even managers who are not going to be responsible for producing financial reports would still be expected to understand any data that is presented as tables, graphs or charts.

How hard will it be?

The difficulty level of the test you take will reflect the level of numerical knowledge needed in the position or place you are applying for. The practice tests in Part 2 of this book span a wide range of difficulty levels. This is deliberate and reflects the range of tests in current usage. Starting with the easiest and getting increasingly difficult the practice questions cover the full range of numerical reasoning ability.

you are not about to sit an A-level Maths test

Remember, you are not about to sit an A-level Maths test. Areas such as complex algebra and the use of mathematical formulae are not included in any of the practice test questions. The more esoteric mathematical operations such as powers, square roots, prime numbers and probabilities will also be avoided for the reason that they rarely appear in numerical reasoning tests.

How can I prepare?

The best way to improve your performance is through practice. Furthermore, you will get the most benefit if you practise with questions that mirror the exact test you are preparing to take.

the best way to improve your performance is through practice

Most of the test questions will be multiple choice. Don't be fooled into thinking that this makes them easier. The answer options are deliberately designed to catch out those who guess or make sloppy errors. If you want to pass, you need to be able to work out the answers.

How important is this test?

Broadly speaking, the earlier in an assessment process that you are being asked to complete a numerical reasoning test the more important it is to pass. Candidates who do not pass are sifted out of the process, allowing employers to focus on applicants whose skills are better suited to the job.

You may be taking a numerical reasoning test as part of an assessment centre where many different types of exercise – such as interviews, group exercises, presentations, role plays and other psychometric tests – are combined. When the test is just one part of several assessments you will not be sifted out on the basis of the numerical reasoning test alone. That said, it is still important to pass – you don't want a poor test performance to let you down.

 recap

- Numerical reasoning testing is now widely used in the application process for many jobs and educational courses.

- Well-designed numerical reasoning tests are used because they predict future performance at work.

- Your numerical reasoning test should mirror the types of calculations and problems that you will encounter in the role that you are applying for.

- There are many different types of numerical reasoning test, at varying levels of difficulty.

- Multiple choice does not mean multiple guess. If you want to pass, you need to be able to work out the answers.

CHAPTER 2

Practice
makes perfect

Try approaching your upcoming numerical reasoning test like a running race. You wouldn't just turn up at the starting line and hope for the best, would you? Instead, you'd go out for training runs in the preceding weeks – starting with easy jogs then building up to faster sprints. On the race day you'd want to be rested, relaxed and in peak physical and mental condition. Putting in plenty of practice in the run up to your test should help you give a winning performance on your test day. So let's get down to work!

Why should I practise?

Practising questions is proven to significantly improve your chances of passing a numerical reasoning test. Try to squeeze in as much advance practice as possible so that you can boost your confidence and keep a clear head on the day. Continually review what you have learnt during practice test sessions so that you use your time more effectively.

> continually review what you have learnt during practice test sessions

When should I practise?

First think about how much time you can spare for practising. Then set aside that time so you can conduct as many practice sessions as possible over a period of several weeks or months. Try to set aside a particular time of day when your mind is most alert.

I'd strongly advise against doing all your preparation in one huge hit. You will learn and retain much more if you undertake several practice sessions instead of one big one. At first it may seem as if you are only making small gains, but these small gains will soon add up to improved numeracy skills.

How much practice do I need?

That depends on why you are taking the test and your current skill level. Your numerical reasoning test may be a key to a new job or a new stage in your life. It is worth maximising your practice opportunities when your future is at stake.

The time required to improve your performance will vary between a few hours for those who are just a little bit rusty to several days for those who haven't used their basic maths skills in a long time.

Where should I start?

If you don't already know exactly what type of numerical reasoning test you will be taking, you should find out as your first step. Knowing what to expect on your test day will give you a big advantage, so learn as much as you can about the test you are going to take. Your recruiting organisation may send you practice material in advance of your test. This may be in the form of sample questions, either online or in printed format. The information should also outline why the test is being used in the process and – most importantly – the exact nature of the test that you will be taking on the day.

This practice opportunity levels the playing field and gives everyone a fair chance – particularly important for people who have not taken a numerical reasoning test before. If this material is not sent to you in advance, contact your prospective employer and ask for information about the test you are going to complete.

Before taking a practice test

- Identify a quiet place to work where you are unlikely to be disturbed. It is important to find an environment where you can work quietly and really concentrate.
- Clear away anything that may distract you before starting.
- Turn your mobile phone off.
- Have a clock or watch handy to time how quickly you work.
- Have plenty of scrap paper available to use.

During the practice test

Research has shown that most people's concentration levels drop off after 40–50 minutes, so you should limit your practice session accordingly. Try to treat your practice session as a real test to help you get into the right mindset. This will help reduce any nerves on the test day.

Timekeeping techniques

It is essential to manage your time efficiently in the run-up to the test to ensure you fit in enough practice sessions. But how you use your time *during* the test is also extremely important, as during the real test you will be working under strictly timed conditions. You don't necessarily need to finish the test in order to pass, but you do need a certain number of correct answers, so it is essential to pace yourself.

> how you use your time *during* the test is extremely important

Right at the start of the test, work out roughly how long you should be spending on each question. Try to ensure that you do not spend longer than this as you work through the questions.

Every 10 minutes or so, quickly check the time remaining against the number of questions that you have left to answer.

It is tempting to be overly cautious. Did the question really say that? What were the units again? You need to cultivate a focused technique that allows you to read the question, memorise what you're being asked to do and then know when you have the required answer.

If you finish the test before the time is up use the remaining time to check your work or return to any questions that you could not answer.

A calculated risk

Many numerical reasoning tests allow you to use a calculator when completing them. On higher-level numerical reasoning tests there will certainly be many questions requiring the use of a calculator. However, don't be tempted to use it on every single question. For time management reasons, only use a calculator if you are likely to make a mistake if you don't use one.

After taking a practice test

● Circle any incorrect answers.

● Go through each answer explanation for those questions you got wrong.

Learn from your mistakes

Pay attention to any errors that you make throughout your practice session. This will help you learn where there are strengths and weaknesses in your numerical reasoning abilities. Are you still struggling with ratios? Or perhaps it's percentages that you are having trouble with?

once you are aware of any weaknesses you can focus future practice sessions on this area

Once you are aware of any weaknesses you can focus future practice sessions on this area.

Stretch yourself

Don't just focus on practice questions that you can do quite easily – stretch yourself with harder questions. Undertake timed practice tests on a regular basis to get your brain used to working under pressure.

Common concerns

How do I know if I am improving?

Effective feedback is the key to improving your overall performance. After each practice session keep a record of how many questions you get right. Compare your performances so you can gauge your improvement over time.

Am I working at a steady pace?

Because most numerical reasoning tests are timed you need to be focused and alert. You obviously need to work accurately as there's no benefit in getting questions wrong. But you also need to work briskly. Remember that someone who gets more questions wrong than you could actually get a better score, simply by also answering more questions correctly!

Am I avoiding careless mistakes?

If you find yourself making too many careless mistakes you clearly need to slow down. Yes, you need to work fast, but the key is to work at a pace that allows you to get questions right. It is also essential to read the question carefully to avoid sloppy mistakes, such as answering in the wrong unit of measurement.

Are any patterns emerging?

Look for trends. Do you tend to make more mistakes at the

beginning of your practice session? This could be a consequence of nerves. You need to work on achieving a high level of focus as soon as you start work.

Are you making more mistakes near the end of your practice session? This could be because you are rushing the last few questions. You need to work steadily and maintain concentration throughout an entire test.

I'm not getting any better

learning from your mistakes is the key to improving

Do you know why you are getting questions wrong? Learning from your mistakes is the key to improving. If you are unaccustomed to a particular type of question it makes sense to spend additional time familiarising yourself with them. Don't assume that you can pass without learning how to answer that sort of question.

The questions are too difficult for me

In order to improve your score you need practice questions that mirror the difficulty level of the actual test you will be taking. The practice tests in Part II increase in difficulty, so start with the easiest questions and work your way up to the more challenging practice tests in subsequent chapters.

If you are finding even the easiest questions difficult it may be a sign that you need to go back to basics. For example, if you are guessing at questions involving percentages then you need to learn how percentages work. Do this before attempting any more practice questions.

 **brilliant** recap

Do

✔ Practise right up to the day before you are going to be taking your test.

✔ Familiarise yourself with the test you will be taking so you can tailor your practice sessions accordingly.

✔ Eliminate distractions so you can concentrate as you practise.

✔ Work at a brisk pace and always keep an eye on the time.

✔ Focus on understanding why you keep getting particular questions wrong and on avoiding any sloppy mistakes.

Don't

✘ Rely on one big practice session. Multiple practice sessions, limited to 40–50 minutes, will be more effective long term.

✘ Make sloppy mistakes. Read the question and answer options carefully.

✘ Go straight to the answers section without attempting to do the practice tests yourself.

✘ Assume that you can pass the test by avoiding the types of question that you find most difficult.

✘ Forget to double-check your answers if time permits.

CHAPTER 3

Brush up your maths skills

H as it been a while since you used basic mental arithmetic? There are many mathematical rules that you probably learnt at school but you may since have forgotten. If your basic maths skills have become a little rusty the following section is designed to help you brush up. In order to pass your test you will need to be able to perform calculations quickly and accurately in your head.

Somewhere, deep inside your mind, your maths knowledge is still there – you just need to brush away the cobwebs. As you work through the practice tests in Part 2 you should

> somewhere, deep inside your mind, your maths knowledge is still there

hopefully find these numerical skills coming back to you. Let's start by ensuring that you have a clear understanding of the following basic maths skills:

1 basic numerical operations;

2 mental maths;

3 the metric system of measurement;

4 more complex mathematical operations.

If you are certain that you have these basics covered then you should skip ahead.

Basic numerical operations

Basic numerical reasoning requires an ability to manipulate numerical information in ways that you will have learnt at school – for example, using the four operators, addition, subtraction, multiplication and division, and the decimal system.

you should definitely
memorise your
multiplication tables

Almost every question that you answer will rely on addition, subtraction, multiplication or division. If you always need to write these calculations down on paper you should definitely memorise your multiplication tables – it will save you time and improve your accuracy. As you probably remember from primary school, this involves rote learning.

Mental maths

When it comes to passing a numerical reasoning test under restricted time conditions, being able to do simple addition, subtraction, multiplication and division in your head will be a huge advantage. It's not a problem if you need to write down long division, as long as you get the decimal columns in the right place!

Let's look at how mental arithmetic can help you work more quickly and efficiently. You probably know that $12 \times 12 = 144$. But you will be able to quickly work out simple calculations in your head if, upon seeing numbers such as 14,400, you also realise that:

- this number is divisible by 12 (and hence also divisible by 6, 4, 3 and 2);
- 14,400 divided by 12 is merely 144 divided by 12 with a couple of zeroes added on the end.

If you know your multiplication tables and the decimal system, large numbers with zeroes at the end shouldn't faze you. You will be expected to be able to work comfortably with large figures in your numerical reasoning test. For example, you need to know the common abbreviations for large numbers, e.g. thousands (1,000s or 000s), tens of thousands (10,000s), hundreds of thousands (100,000s) and millions (i.e. 1,000,000s).

The metric system of measurement

The international metric system is based on multiples of 10. For example, 10 mm = 1 cm. The metric system covers the weight measures of milligrams (mg), grams (g) and kilograms (kg); the distance measures of millimetre (mm), centimetre (cm), metre (m) and kilometre (km); and speed (km per hour). You need to be able to convert across all measurement terms that are in common usage within the metric system, for example 1,000 grams = 1 kilogram. You also need to know how to convert from one measurement to another. For example, since 60 minutes is the same as an hour, then 120 minutes is 2 hours; 101 pence is £1.01, and so on. Don't be caught out by the simple mistake of answering in the wrong units!

> don't be caught out by the simple mistake of answering in the wrong units

Here are some of the basic numeracy measurements that you need to be able to work with on a numerical reasoning test:

1   the 24-hour clock, e.g. 13:00 for one o'clock in the afternoon;

2   weight measurements (kg, g);

3   £ and pence;

4   distance (cm, m, miles and km);

5   speeds (km per hour and mph);

6   volume (1,000 millilitres = 1 litre).

Two of the commonest measurements that you are likely to encounter in a numerical reasoning test are the UK monetary system (£ and pence) and time intervals [hours (hr), minutes (min), seconds (sec)], including the 24-hour clock.

Complex mathemetical operations

Here are some of the more complex mathematical operations that you will need to be able to perform:

- ratios;
- fractions;
- percentages;
- decimals and decimal places;
- exchange rates;
- averages (means) and frequencies; (some tests also expect you to work with medians and modes);
- rounding up numbers.

You will need to demonstrate an effective working knowledge of many of these in any numerical reasoning test, and your performance will probably improve if you can work with them in your head.

Remember that when you have to carry out a string of computations, the multiplication and division calculations take precedence over any addition and subtraction calculations. This is shown in the written form by the use of brackets around the multiplication and division calculations.

geometry, prime numbers and calculus are unlikely to appear in a numerical reasoning test

You may (or may not!) be pleased to know that geometry, prime numbers and calculus are unlikely to appear in a numerical reasoning test because they are not commonly used in the workplace.

Expressing numbers in different ways

You need to be comfortable with moving between different ways of expressing numbers – for example, changing a number into a percentage or changing a figure shown with decimal places into a fraction. Fractions, decimal points and percentages are just different ways of splitting a number down into smaller divisions. You can think of these as interchangeable. I've given a few examples below (in order of increasing size).

Common fractions	Decimal (two decimal places – after the decimal point)	Percentage or % (of the number 1)
1/10	0.10	10%
1/5	0.20	20%
1/4	0.25	25%
1/2	0.50	50%
3/4	0.75	75%

If you work best with a particular format, say percentages, then – given the time restrictions on any test – it makes sense for you to use your preference wherever possible. In other words, if you know straight away that 25% is a ¼ of something you can quickly calculate a division by 4 instead of doing the standard percentage calculation.

The tests in Part 2 of this book will help you practise expressing numbers in different ways. The detailed answer explanations may tell you to calculate the lowest common denominator, and this book assumes that you have a working knowledge of such concepts. However, if you need a reminder of what a common denominator is, or if you need to refresh your understanding of decimal points, percentages, the metric system or the 24-hour clock, there are many helpful websites providing support.

Working it out

The more complex numerical reasoning questions require the use of a calculator and rough paper for writing down the results of the different calculation stages.

always have plenty of rough paper to use

Always have plenty of rough paper to use. When doing the test for real your rough work will not form part of the assessment. It is important to write the question number next to your workings out. That way you are able to return quickly to your calculation if you:

- decide to move on to a different question before reaching the final answer;
- need to use the same early stages of a complex calculation for a subsequent question;
- want to check your answer because it's not shown as one of the answer options;
- need to establish which stage of your calculation is most likely to contain an error.

Interpreting graphs

Whenever you are presented with a graph or table you will need to interpret this quickly and accurately in order to answer the questions efficiently. It is worth giving the graph or table a quick scan – paying particular attention to the axes – before going on to read the first question.

You need to practise interpreting the following:

- *Value of points shown on graphs.* This requires reading both the horizontal and vertical axes on a graph. Each of these is commonly divided into segments and will be labelled accordingly. For example, if the graphical axis starts at zero then goes up to 10, then 20, then 30 and so on you know that the divisions on the axis are in blocks of 10.

● *Axis titles and keys on graphs.* For example, a graph that measures *Cost (in £100s)* will provide points on a graph that are a measure of cost in £s. Each figure represents hundreds, so a figure 3 as represented by the graph is being used to represent £300.

If you are worried about pie charts then just think of the different 'pie segments' as fractions of the total value shown.

Seven speedy short cuts

When working with figures and numerical information there are many useful techniques for improving the speed with which you can manipulate figures. Here are some handy tips that will help you to save time and reduce your calculator usage.

1 When multiplying large figures, ignore the zeroes and work only with the non-zero figures. So if you need to multiply 22,000 by 5 it is quicker to multiply 22 (the non-zero figures) by 5 = 110. You then add the zeroes back on to the answer = 110,000. This technique can also be applied to save time when adding, subtracting or dividing large figures. To subtract 200 from 5,000 you simply ignore the zeroes that are common to both figures. The subtraction then becomes 50 − 2 = 48. Then add the zeroes back on and the answer is 4,800.

2 If you need to multiply by 10, 100 or 1,000 the quickest way to do this is to adjust the number of decimal places. For example, to multiply 67.3 metres by 10, move the decimal point one place to the right ... so 67.3 becomes 673 metres. Similarly, if you are being asked to multiply a figure by 100 or 1,000 you move the decimal points two or three places to the right, respectively.

3 When dividing by 10, 100 or 1,000 the quickest way to do this is to adjust the number of decimal places. For instance,

if you want to divide $99.90 by 10, move the decimal point one place to the left. So $99.90 becomes $9.99. To divide a figure by 100 or 1,000 just move the decimal points two or three places to the left, respectively.

4   When asked to work with numbers that are close to being a 10, 100 or 1,000, you can round up. You may already do this when you go shopping – for example, you may round up an item costing £3.99 to £4.00. Just remember that you have added 1 pence on to the figure and then take account of this fact in your final answer. So if a question concerns the cost of two items costing £3.99 you can calculate 2 × £4.00 = £8.00 then subtract 2 pence (1 pence for each item) and the total cost = £8.00 − 2 pence = £7.98.

5   It is sometimes simpler to 'ignore' the decimal places in the figures that you are manipulating. All that you need to do is to check that your answer has the same number of decimal places as the figures that you started off with. For example, 1.2 (one decimal place) × 1.5 (one decimal place) becomes 12 × 15 = 180. Now remember that the answer will need to have two decimal places, i.e. 1.80. This is a great time-saver, but it is essential to put the decimal point back in the right place!

6   When adding or subtracting large numbers you can just work with the unit numbers (the number furthest to the right, e.g. the 2 on 512) to eliminate some of the multiple choice answer options. For example, 542 + 53 + 444 results in an answer that has the unit number 9, because adding 2 (at the end of 542) to 3 (at the end of 53) and 4 (at the end of 444) equals 9. You can disregard any answer option that does not end in 9.

7   When you manipulate two or more even numbers (any number ending in 2, 4, 6, 8 or 0) your answer will also be an even number. Whether you add, subtract, divide or

multiply two or more even numbers your answer must end in a number 0, 2, 4, 6 or 8. This is one of those bits of knowledge that is useful when working under time pressure in a test, because you can ignore any multiple choice answer options that are not even numbers.

What if my answer just looks wrong?

There are certain things that may indicate that you have made an error somewhere in your calculation. For example, reaching a:

1 *Negative answer.* It is unlikely that the correct answer will be what is called a negative number, i.e. less than zero. In this book you will only see negative values in some answer explanations to represent a decrease over a period of time. For example, a drop of 5% in sales one month could be expressed as – 5%.

2 *Unfeasibly high number,* such as millions of pounds. Questions with charts or tables containing figures of this magnitude usually indicate the scale of the figures with appropriate annotation, such as, *in 000,000s.*

3 *Smaller or larger number than the figures given in the question.* Quickly check the scale of the answer you have calculated. If there are single numbers, tens, hundreds or thousands in the data given then the answer should be in a similar scale.

4 If your *answer just looks wrong* you will probably have to start the question again, taking care to recheck the information given, or go back to the last stage of the calculation that you know was correct.

   – One helpful short cut is to just check the single figures at the end of the numbers that you have manipulated to reach your answer. For example, if the question is 345 × 3 then the answer has to end in a 5 because

(34)$5 \times 3 = --5$. This at least allows you to exclude any multiple choice answer options that do not end in 5.

Other ways to improve

take advantage of any opportunity to brush up on your application of simple mathematical operations

There are lots of everyday situations where you can practise your numeracy skills. Take advantage of any opportunity to brush up on your application of simple mathematical operations (addition, subtraction, multiplication, division). These activities will improve your mental agility in tandem with working your way through the practice questions.

- When you are at the supermarket, try keeping a running tally in your head of the items you intend to purchase.

- When you dine at a restaurant, use mental arithmetic to calculate what you should leave as a tip. Try working out the service charge at different percentages. If splitting the bill with friends, do the division in your head. When paying, quickly work out how much change you should receive.

- Your daily newspaper offers many great ways to sharpen your numeracy skills. When, looking at the weather report, try switching the temperatures between Fahrenheit and Celsius. Check out the previous day's share movements. Imagine if you had invested £1,000 in one of the shares listed. How much would you have gained or lost yesterday? When you see complex tables and graphs of statistical data, spend time reviewing the axes of the graph and the headings of the table.

- Go through some of your old bank statements or telephone bills. Sum up the individual entries in as fast a time as possible by rounding up the decimal places.

- When you are playing – or watching – sports where there are high scores involved, such as darts and snooker, try to track the scores in your head.

Although beneficial, these everyday activities are not as important as working through the practice questions in Part II of this book. If you find that your mathematical skills are very rusty an evening class in maths would be a good way to get help. Further education colleges routinely offer courses in numeracy skills.

 **brilliant** recap

- You need to understand basic maths operations before moving on to more complex calculations.
- Use as many short cuts and time-saving techniques as you can.
- Make sure to read each question carefully to ensure that you are clear about the unit of measurement that the answer requires.
- Avoid sloppy mistakes, such as misplaced decimal points.
- Memorise your times tables by writing them down as quickly as possible or reciting them out loud.
- Look for opportunities to improve your numeracy in your daily life.

CHAPTER 4

Succeed on
test day

Hopefully you have now had a chance to practise your numeracy skills and are feeling ready to put your test-taking strategies into action. But before that, let's have a look at the test-taking process in general. Being fully aware of what to expect on your test day will help allay any jitters.

> being fully aware of what to expect on your test day will help allay any jitters

What will I be told in advance?

You should have been provided with the following information, in keeping with best practice:

- logistical information, such as directions about how to get to the test centre;
- advance notice that you will be taking a numerical reasoning test, including the length of time that the test will take to complete;
- an explanation of the testing process;
- the part that the test will play in the overall process, including who will have access to your results;
- any feedback arrangements.

If you feel that anything has not been adequately explained to you, or if you are uncomfortable with any aspect of these issues, then don't hesitate to get a contact name from your prospective employer or place of study.

Ensuring fairness

if you have a disability, then be sure to inform your prospective employer or educational establishment in advance

If you have a disability then be sure to inform your prospective employer or educational establishment in advance if you require any adaptations to the testing process. It is likely that you would have been asked this question on your application form. You may also have been asked to complete a separate equal opportunities or monitoring form. Let them know how you have approached testing in the past and what provisions need to be made to ensure that you have equal access to the numerical reasoning test. This includes the format of the test, the medium through which it is communicated and how it is communicated. The testing process can be adapted whenever it is appropriate to do so, including an additional time allowance and having the questions delivered in Braille or large print.

Mental preparation

If you have completed plenty of practice questions and familiarised yourself with your test format you should be feeling confident. When you take your test you need to be able to concentrate 100 per cent and maintain a positive, confident mindset.

channel your energy in a positive way

Instead of worrying, channel your energy in a positive way – by applying useful strategies and working briskly through the questions.

Physical preparation

Mental preparation isn't enough – you need to prepare yourself physically, too. Try to get a good night's sleep before the test as you will concentrate better if you are fully rested. If you've done your mental preparation in advance, you don't need to stay up all night 'cramming'!

Test-taking tactics

Remember that you are not expected to get a perfect score. Even if you get several answers wrong you can still pass the test, as long as a relatively

> you are not expected to get a perfect score

small number of incorrect answers is outweighed by a much larger number of correct answers. Here are some top test-taking tactics to help you maximise your performance.

- Be methodical and do not jump ahead. Start by looking at the first question, answer it and then move on to the next. It is important to concentrate your mind on one question at a time.

- Don't lose any marks for interpreting the information given incorrectly. Read each question very carefully and always check that you have read across tables, charts and graphs correctly.

- Rely on your intuition if you can't decide between two answers.

- If you run out of time or you cannot answer some questions properly you have nothing to lose by putting down an educated guess. The only exception is if your test is being negatively marked (meaning that you would lose a mark for getting each question wrong).

Reviewing your answer options

When doing a multiple-choice numerical reasoning test, ruling out one or two answer options reduces the number of correct answer possibilities. As you complete the test, ask yourself a few questions:

● Are any of the answer options unfeasible? If you have started the numerical calculation in your head, are any of these answer options not of the scale that you expect? If you are going to guess, you have more chance of being correct if you have already ruled out some of the answers.

● Are any answer options deliberately designed to mislead you? Some answer options may look very similar to the correct answer – for example, a slightly higher or lower value, or a decimal point in a different position. Take care not to be caught out.

● Follow your intuition if you have a bad feeling about your answer. Just because it is one of the multiple-choice options does not necessarily mean that it is the right answer. If in doubt, double check your work.

What if I get stuck?

don't get bogged down

If you find that you are spending too long on a particular question, don't get bogged down. We all come across questions that we find difficult. The quicker you decide to cut your losses the better, since that will give you more time to work on questions that you find easier. Give your best guess and move on. Mark the question so that you can go back at the end of the test and finish it off if time allows.

Online testing

Online testing has been the dominant testing medium for the past few years. One leading test publisher now only publishes its psychometric tests online. Today, the job application process is likely to involve completing an online application form and uploading your CV to an online testing site. All of this digital information immediately becomes available to your potential employer. For high-volume recruitment processes, such as graduate-entry training schemes, a numerical reasoning test is almost always one of the initial sifts – regardless of the position applied for. The streamlining of applicant processing has shifted modern recruitment away from old-fashioned, labour-intensive paper-based processes.

There are a few major differences when taking an online test as opposed to a traditional paper and pencil test:

1 You will not have a test administrator available to answer any questions or to manage any problems. An online contact will be made available for you to use, so it's vital that you take your online test on a computer that has a reliable broadband connection.

2 The functionality of some online tests is fixed so that you cannot go back to a previous question.

3 Most online tests require you to enter an answer for each question, otherwise you cannot progress to the next question.

It's always best to practise with test questions that are as similar as possible to those in your real test. Once you have found out who publishes the test you will be taking, visit their website so you can practise with the questions they provide. Kenexa IBM, for example, offer a wide range of practice test examples on their website: www.kenexa.com/Solutions/Assessments/AssessmentGuidance. The author's company website also has some common test examples (www.robwilliamsassessment.co.uk).

Other tips for taking online tests

Whilst most online tests for recruitment purposes are completed at home, you are advised to make your home environment as professional as possible. Take the test when you are best able to concentrate and focus without any interruptions. Even a short lapse in concentration could reduce your score by a couple of marks – potentially the difference between a pass and a fail.

> take the test when you are best able to concentrate and focus without any interruptions

- You are allowed as much time as you like to read the instructions onscreen, so make sure that you are absolutely clear on what you are being asked to do.

- You will be the only person in the room, but that doesn't mean that you control the time allowed on the test. Once you have started you need to complete the test in the allocated time. You can take a break whenever you need to, but it will cost you valuable time.

- A well-designed online test will have been thoroughly tested to work on most computers. You should be told any technical requirements in advance. But if you do have an access problem at any stage, use the contact information provided.

- If you do not have internet access at home, think about alternative venues for taking the test. For example, you could complete the test on a friend or relative's computer or at your local library.

- Don't leave taking the test to the last minute in case you run into any computer problems.

Adaptive tests

The leading test publishers typically offer adaptive online numerical reasoning tests. Adaptive tests are shorter since they have been designed to measure your numeracy skills as efficiently as possible. As the name implies, online adaptive test questions deliberately adapt to how you are performing as you progress through the test. You answer the first question and if it is correct you will then get a more difficult question. However, if you get it wrong, you will be presented with an easier question. This type of test can feel challenging since, as the questions get progressively harder, you are being pushed until you reach the highest level at which you can answer questions correctly. Using this process and some complicated statistical analysis, an adaptive test determines the optimal questions to ask each candidate.

Are there any benefits for me?

- Adaptive testing has led to a reduction from typically 25–30 minutes to 15–20 minutes for some online numerical reasoning tests. So you can complete the test in less time.
- The online test will have a timer visible throughout which makes it easy for you to track your progress.
- Traditional tests present you with a range of easy, medium and difficult test questions. When you take an adaptive test, however, after the first few questions you will find that the questions are matched roughly to your numerical ability level.

How will my test results be used?

Your prospective employer or place of study expects that there will be a range of test scores on the numerical reasoning test. That's why the test is being used in the first place – to differentiate between applicants in terms of their numerical ability.

A few comparisons will be made:

1   Each individual's overall score is compared to those of a large group of hundreds – sometimes thousands – of similar

applicants who have taken the same test before. This is the norm group – the normal range of scores that are typical of the type of people who sit the test. This way, your individual score is given in a meaningful way for that particular test.

2   At the same time, there is a group of applicants who took the test around the same time as you did. The pass mark is also likely to be based on how those other applicants performed. It may go up or down depending on the number of vacancies for a particular job or course or on the number of people who have applied.

3   Few people achieve the maximum mark for this norm group. This reflects the fact that you are not necessarily expected to finish the test in the time available and are not expected to receive full marks.

> your numerical reasoning test may be one stage in a long recruitment process

Your numerical reasoning test may be one stage in a long recruitment process. It will be used to screen out unsuitable applicants who do not have the necessary level of numeracy skills. This process is called a sifting out, or deselection, process.

Will I get any feedback?

Feedback should always be provided and may take several forms. Remember that it is your relative performance that has been measured – meaning how your performance compared to those of the large norm group that have taken the test previously. You won't receive marks out of ten, or a percentage score, as you might expect. Instead, your feedback could be one of the following:

● *A standardised score such as a percentile.* This is similar to a percentage, but a percentile of 60 per cent means that you did better than 60 per cent of the norm group.

- *A band that compares you to the norm group* – e.g. average or above average. Remember, the term 'average' refers to average within a group of people *similar to you* who have taken the test for similar reasons to yourself. Your results are not being compared to those of the general population. So, a 'slightly below average' or 'below average' grade does not mean that you are worse than everyone else in the general population.

Good luck!

By now, you hopefully know what to expect from your numerical reasoning test and have had plenty of opportunity to practise. As you've seen, there are a lot of different strategies that you can apply to test-taking in general and numerical questions specifically. If you want a quick and easy way to remember some key points that have been covered, just think of the Three Big Cs:

- concentration;
- confidence;
- continual practice.

 brilliant recap

- If you have special needs, get in touch with the contact provided well in advance of your test day.
- Don't make any assumptions - if anything is unclear check before proceeding. The administrator is there to answer your questions.
- Remember that all questions are worth the same. The important thing is to answer as many correctly as you can.
- Only guess on questions that you have no possibility of answering correctly.
- Feedback should always be provided and can take different forms. It compares your performance to that of a norm group.

Time to practise

This part of the book is all about practising. And not just any practice, but *targeted* practice, using test questions similar to the actual test you will be taking. Whether you've got months to prepare for your numerical reasoning test, or just a few days, be sure to schedule in as much practice as possible. It's worth putting in the effort when entry to a future profession is at stake. In addition to the practice test questions and answer explanations there are lots of helpful hints, tips and strategies scattered throughout Part 2. Be sure to read them as they suggest great ways to improve your overall performance.

Psychometric testing is a constantly evolving field and employers regularly update the tests they use in recruitment. So the practice tests in Part 2 do not mirror the exact format of any specific numerical reasoning tests. Instead, they are arranged in a rough order of increasing difficulty. As a benchmark, the practice tests featured in Chapter 5 are at a level equivalent to the numerical reasoning questions you would find on a test to enter the armed services. The questions in Chapter 8 are on a par with those featured in the UKCAT, the UK medical school admission test. The most advanced practice tests in Chapters 9 and 10 are similar to those commonly used during the graduate recruitment process. Before tackling Part 2 it would be wise to find out exactly what type and level of numerical reasoning test you will be taking.

At the end of each practice test you will find the answers, as well as detailed step-by-step calculations where necessary. Don't be tempted to simply study the answer explanations, however. You won't get the full benefit of a practice session without actually attempting to answer the questions yourself!

If the practice questions you started with are too difficult you can always go back to complete the earlier chapters. Equally, feel free to skip ahead if you find the questions too easy. Stretch yourself by trying practice tests in subsequent chapters – the harder questions will help sharpen your numerical abilities. And if you are finding it easy to answer the questions correctly, challenge yourself by attempting to improve your speed.

Good luck!

CHAPTER 5

Basic numerical
reasoning tests

Introduction to this format

Tests of basic numeracy are one of the most basic forms of numerical reasoning test. Typically, these are *one calculation* maths tests akin to those you would have done in school.

Guidance for basic numerical reasoning tests

The practice questions appear in sets of 20 questions. Each of these is followed by their respective 20 answer explanations. You are advised to:

- allow yourself 6–8 minutes to complete each set of 20 questions;
- check your answers against the answer explanations that follow the test once you have completed all 20 questions;
- do this before you move on to the next test so that you can apply anything you have learnt immediately – this will aid your memory.

---

brilliant example – Armed services

When joining any of the armed services – for example to become an Army soldier or officer – you will need to take a verbal reasoning test. It tests your ability to process information, identify relationships and differentiate between relevant and irrelevant information. The reasoning test features ▶

several different types of questions – verbal reasoning, spatial reasoning and abstract reasoning – as well as numerical reasoning. It does not require the use of a calculator. This is a test of how quickly and accurately you can complete basic mathematical operations, such as addition, subtraction, multiplication and division. The test also requires you to show that you can quickly and accurately use fractions, percentages and basic algebra.

brilliant tips

● Focus on working accurately while also trying to complete as many questions as you can.

● You need to be able to complete roughly two to three questions on average in a minute. Time yourself and see how close you are to achieving this benchmark.

● It is better to guess than to leave a question unanswered as you do not lose marks for an incorrect answer.

Basic numeracy practice test 1

1   What is the number 55.368 to two decimal places?
    (A) 55.30
    (B) 55.35
    (C) 55.36
    (D) 55.37
    (E) 55.40

2   Add 456 to 9,322
    (A) 9,678
    (B) 9,687
    (C) 9,778
    (D) 9,787
    (E) 9,788

3   What is 40% of 5,000?
    (A) 2,000
    (B) 2,500
    (C) 3,000
    (D) 3,500
    (E) 4,000

4   A garden measures 20 metres by 15 metres. What is the area
    of the garden, in square metres?
    (A) 150 square metres
    (B) 200 square metres
    (C) 250 square metres
    (D) 300 square metres
    (E) 350 square metres

5   Subtract 99.1 from 144.9.
    (A) 45.9
    (B) 45.8
    (C) 45.7
    (D) 45.6
    (E) 45.5

6   What is 0.40 expressed as a percentage of 1?
    (A) 4%
    (B) 14%
    (C) 24%
    (D) 34%
    (E) 40%

7   17.5% of the cost of buying a new printer is VAT. If a new printer costs £50.00 without VAT then how much is the VAT?
    (A) £8.75
    (B) £17.50
    (C) £50.00
    (D) £58.75
    (E) £67.50

8    $77 \times 3 = ?$
    (A) 211
    (B) 221
    (C) 231
    (D) 241
    (E) 251

9   A ninth of a family's monthly budget is spent on gas and electricity bills. If the average cost per month of gas and electricity bills is £90 then how much is the monthly budget.
    (A) £800.00
    (B) £810.00
    (C) £890.00
    (D) £900.00
    (E) £990.00

10   What is 40% of 500?
    (A) 100
    (B) 150
    (C) 200
    (D) 250
    (E) 300

11   0.25 × 2.6 = ?
   (A) 0.69
   (B) 0.68
   (C) 0.67
   (D) 0.66
   (E) 0.65

12   A salesman leaves his house at 9:00 and travels 100 miles to get to his client meeting at 11:00. What is his average speed?
   (A) 35 mph
   (B) 40 mph
   (C) 45 mph
   (D) 50 mph
   (E) 55 mph

13   What is the number 15.6844 to three decimal places?
   (A) 15.680
   (B) 15.684
   (C) 15.685
   (D) 15.690
   (E) 15.700

14   What is 0.40 expressed as a fraction?
   (A) $\frac{4}{5}$
   (B) $\frac{3}{5}$
   (C) $\frac{2}{5}$
   (D) $\frac{1}{5}$
   (E) $\frac{1}{10}$

15   200 × 0.25 = ?
   (A) 50
   (B) 55
   (C) 60
   (D) 65
   (E) 70

16 $\frac{1}{3} \times \frac{1}{8} = ?$

   (A) $\frac{2}{3}$

   (B) $\frac{1}{3}$

   (C) $\frac{2}{8}$

   (D) $\frac{1}{8}$

   (E) $\frac{1}{24}$

17 What is 70% expressed as a decimal?

   (A) 0.9

   (B) 0.8

   (C) 0.7

   (D) 0.6

   (E) 0.5

18 What is 0.10 expressed as a fraction?

   (A) $\frac{1}{4}$

   (B) $\frac{1}{5}$

   (C) $\frac{1}{8}$

   (D) $\frac{1}{10}$

   (E) $\frac{1}{100}$

19 $410 \times 80 = ?$

   (A) 3,280

   (B) 3,820

   (C) 32,800

   (D) 38,200

   (E) 38,800

20 A woman works a seven-hour day five days of the week and then works 3 hours' overtime over the weekend. What is the total number of hours that she works that week?

   (A) 38

   (B) 39

   (C) 40

   (D) 41

   (E) 42

Review your answers to practice test 1

1 (D) 55.37

   Review the third figure after the decimal point.

   This is greater than 5 so the second figure after the decimal point needs to be rounded up.

2 (C) 9,778

3 (A) $100 \times 40/5,000 = 2,000$

4 (D) 20 metres $\times$ 15 metres = 300 square metres

5 (B) 45.8

6 (E) $100 \times 0.4/1 = 40\%$

7 (A) £50.00 $\times$ 17.5/100 = £8.75

8 (C) 231

9 (B) 9 $\times$ average utilities bill = 9 $\times$ £90 = £810

10 (C) $500 \times 40/100 = 200$

11 (E) 0.65

12 (D) 50 miles per hour

   Step 1: Calculate the time taken:
   11:00 hrs – 9:00 represents 2 hours

   Step 2: Calculate the average speed:
   average speed = distance/time taken = 100 miles/2 hours
   = 50 mph

13 (B) 15.684
   Review 4th decimal place.
   4th decimal place is less than 5 so the third figure after the decimal point needs to be rounded down.

14 (C) $\frac{2}{5}$

15 (A) 50

16 (E) $\frac{1}{3} \times \frac{1}{8} = (\frac{1}{3} \times 8) = \frac{1}{24}$

17 (C) $\frac{70}{100} = 0.7$

18 (D) $\frac{1}{10}$

19 (C) 32,800

20 (A) 38 hours

Step 1: Calculate the hours during the week:
$7 \times 5 = 35$ hours

Step 2: Add weekend hours:
total hours $= 35 + 3 = 38$ hours

Basic numeracy practice test 2

1   $50 \times 0.5 = ?$

(A) 15

(B) 20

(C) 25

(D) 30

(E) 35

2   $0.98 + 0.47 = ?$

(A) 1.48

(B) 1.47

(C) 1.46

(D) 1.45

(E) 1.44

3   $432 + 88 = ?$

(A) 520

(B) 516

(C) 513

(D) 510

(E) 500

4   $12 \times 200 = ?$

(A) 2,300

(B) 2,400

(C) 2,500

(D) 2,600

(E) 2,700

5   $0.66 - 0.23 = ?$

(A) 0.53

(B) 0.51

(C) 0.48

(D) 0.43

(E) 0.33

6   $\frac{1}{3} \times 33 = ?$

   (A) 11

   (B) 13

   (C) 15

   (D) 18

   (E) 23

7   $225 - 44 = ?$

   (A) 197

   (B) 191

   (C) 187

   (D) 181

   (E) 177

8   $0.5 \times 36 = ?$

   (A) 14

   (B) 16

   (C) 18

   (D) 20

   (E) 22

9   $15 \times \frac{1}{3} = ?$

   (A) 4

   (B) 5

   (C) 6

   (D) 7

   (E) 8

10 $0.45 \times 200 = ?$

   (A) 70

   (B) 75

   (C) 80

   (D) 85

   (E) 90

11 What is 31.456 expressed to two decimal places?

   (A) 31.40

(B) 31.45
(C) 31.46
(D) 31.50
(E) 31.60

12 $\frac{1}{3} + \frac{1}{2} = ?$
   (A) $\frac{7}{9}$
   (B) $\frac{7}{8}$
   (C) $\frac{5}{6}$
   (D) $\frac{4}{6}$
   (E) $\frac{2}{3}$

13 $46/4.6 = ?$
   (A) 4
   (B) 6
   (C) 8
   (D) 10
   (E) 12

14 $\frac{1}{4} \times 600 = ?$
   (A) 125
   (B) 150
   (C) 175
   (D) 200
   (E) 225

15 $0.25 \times 0.5 = ?$
   (A) 0.120
   (B) 0.125
   (C) 0.130
   (D) 0.135
   (E) 0.140

16 $90 + 0.99 = ?$
   (A) 90.09
   (B) 90.90
   (C) 90.99

(D) 99.09
(E) 99.99

17 550/11 = ?
   (A) 50
   (B) 49
   (C) 48
   (D) 47
   (E) 46

18 5.5 × 9.5 = ?
   (A) 51.25
   (B) 51.75
   (C) 52.25
   (D) 52.50
   (E) 52.75

19 ¼ × 500 = ?
   (A) 125
   (B) 150
   (C) 175
   (D) 200
   (E) 225

20 What is 30% of 250?
   (A) 60
   (B) 65
   (C) 70
   (D) 75
   (E) 80

Review your answers to practice test 2

1   (C) $50 \times 0.5 = 25$

2   (D) $0.98 + 0.47 = 1.45$

3   (A) $432 + 88 = 520$

4   (B) $12 \times 200 = 2,400$

5   (D) $0.66 - 0.23 = 0.43$

6   (A) $\frac{1}{3} \times 33 = 11$

7   (D) $225 - 44 = 181$

8   (C) $0.5 \times 36 = 18$

9   (B) $15 \times \frac{1}{3} = 5$

10   (E) $0.45 \times 200 = 90$

11   (C) 31.456 expressed to two decimal places $= 31.46$

12   (C) $\frac{1}{3} + \frac{1}{2} = \frac{5}{6}$

13   (D) $46/4.6 = 10$

14   (B) $\frac{1}{4} \times 600 = 150$

15   (B) $0.25 \times 0.5 = 0.125$

16   (C) $90 + 0.99 = 90.99$

17   (A) $550/11 = 50$

18   (C) $5.5 \times 9.5 = 52.25$

19   (A) $\frac{1}{4} \times 500 = 125$

20   (D) $30\% \times 250 = 75$

CHAPTER 6

Numerical
comprehension
tests

Introduction to this format

This type of numerical reasoning question is slightly more difficult than those given in the previous chapter. In this chapter the questions are sentence-based, requiring you to extract the appropriate calculation from the information given. More complex questions based on tables and graphs can be found in the chapters that follow.

brilliant example – Graduate milk round

The 'milk round' is a metaphor traditionally used in the UK to describe the process of companies visiting universities each year to advertise the opportunities available and recruit graduates – the metaphor being based on Britain's long-standing door-to-door milk delivery service. Recruiters are generally large business organisations with their own in-house graduate trainee schemes. Since the late 1990s this process of physically visiting universities has given way to an online version where graduates can research training schemes and apply for jobs.

Graduate aptitude tests have always formed some part of the graduate recruitment process but, in recent years, with the dramatic increase in numbers of graduates, their use has become more widespread as an effective way for companies to assess large numbers of graduates. Numerical reasoning tests are commonly used both as a means of selecting graduates for interview and as a part of the interview process.

▶

There are many websites that offer free practice opportunities for this popular test format. Search under 'numerical reasoning test practice' and take your pick.

Guidance for numerical comprehension tests

The practice questions appear in sets of 10 questions. Each of these is followed by their respective 10-answer explanations. You are advised to:

- allow yourself 3–4 minutes to complete each set of 10 questions;
- read each question carefully – twice if necessary;
- choose the correct answer from the multiple-choice options shown;
- check your answers against the answer explanations that follow the test once you have completed all 10 questions;
- do this before you move on to the next test so that you can apply anything you have learnt immediately to aid your memory;
- use a calculator to answer the questions.

brilliant tips

- Keep things simple whenever possible so that you can focus on getting the calculation correct.
- Don't be distracted by complex business language, the size of the figures or the measurement units. Nine times out of ten the measurement units will be constant throughout the question and answer.
- If you can get the right answer by doing a rough calculation then by all means do so.

Numerical comprehension practice test 1

1   A financial company's balance sheet includes property assets of £212 million and £40 million in derivative assets. What is the effect on the balance sheet of the property assets rising by a quarter and the derivative assets dropping by three tenths?
(A) £265 million lower
(B) £41 million lower
(C) £12 million lower
(D) £41 million higher
(E) £265 million higher

2   The sales of a multinational company are $480,000 in the Asia-Pacific region and $440,000 in the European region. If the total world-wide sales are $1,150,000 what fraction do these two regions combined represent?
(A) ⅕
(B) ⅖
(C) ⅗
(D) ⅔
(E) ⅘

3   The total regional assets of a global oil company are $950 million in North America and $178 million in Canada. What percentage are these combined regional assets of the total global assets of $9,400 million?
(A) 9.4%
(B) 10%
(C) 10.4%
(D) 12%
(E) 12.4%

4   A transatlantic company's quarterly costs are $48,000 in their sales division and $64,000 in their marketing division. What is the ratio of the sales to marketing costs?
(A) 2:3

(B) 3:2

(C) 3:4

(D) 4:3

(E) 3:5

5   The global marketplace for outsourcing has been predicted to grow from £234,000 million in 2008 to £319,000 million in 2011. What is the total % increase predicted to be over these three years (to one decimal place)?

(A) None of these

(B) 2.1%

(C) 24.2%

(D) 36.3%

(E) 48.4%

6   In an employee survey of 225 employees the response rate was six out of 10. How many employees did not complete the survey?

(A) 40

(B) 60

(C) 90

(D) 135

(E) Can't tell

7   A company pays an interim dividend of 6.2p per company share. A shareholder has 3,250 shares. What is the total value of their interim dividend payment?

(A) £201.50

(B) £211.50

(C) £325.00

(D) £2,015.00

(E) £3,250.00

8   An Internet company pays corporation tax at 21%. If the amount of corporation tax paid is £143,850 how much are the company's taxable profits (in £1,000s)?

(A) 80

(B) 600

(C) 650

(D) 680

(E) 685

9   Market expectations are that a house builder's annual profits
    will fall by 35%. If the previous year's annual profits were
    £4.6 million what are the expected profits for the current
    year (in £100,000s)?
    (A) 29.70
    (B) 29.90
    (C) 30.10
    (D) 2.97
    (E) 2.99

10 In France the monthly sales of a new cosmetics product
    were €60,600. If the sales in Germany and Spain were each
    a third of this, what were the total sales across the three
    European countries (in euros)?
    (A) 101,000
    (B) 100,000
    (C) 91,000
    (D) 11,000
    (E) 10,100

Review your answers to practice test 1

1   **Answer (D) is correct: £41 million higher**
    £212 million $\times$ ¼ = £53 million
    £40 million $\times$ 30/100 = £12 million
    £53 million − £12 million = £41 million

2   **Answer (E) is correct: ⁴/₅**
    $480,000 + $440,000 = $920,000
    $920,000/$1,150,000 = 920/1,150 = ⁴/₅

3   **Answer (D) is correct: 12%**
    $950 million + $178 million = $1,128 million
    $1,128 million/$9,400 million $\times$ 100% = 12%

4   **Answer (C) is correct: 3:4**
    £48,000:£64,000 = 3:4

5   **Answer (D) is correct: 36.3%**
    £319,000 million − £234,000 million = £85 million
    £85 million/£234,000 million $\times$ 100% = 36.3%

6   **Answer (C) is correct: 90**
    100% − 60% = 40% of employees did not complete the
    survey
    225 $\times$ 40/100 = 90 employees

7   **Answer (A) is correct: £201.50**
    6.2p $\times$ 3,250 shares = £201.50

8   **Answer (E) is correct: 685 (in £1000s)**
    £143,850 = 21%
    100% = 100 $\times$ 143,850/21 = 685,000

9   **Answer (B) is correct: 29.90 (in £100,000s)**
    £4.6 million $\times$ 65/100 = £2.99 million

10 **Answer (A) is correct: 101,000**
    French monthly sales = €60,600
    German sales = €20,200
    Spanish sales = €20,200
    Total sales across the three European countries (in euros)
    = 60,600 + 20,200 + 20,200

Numerical comprehension practice test 2

1   A multinational shipping company has annual profits of $42.6 million. What is this in £ (at an exchange rate of $1.40 to the £)?

(A) £300 million

(B) £30.61 million

(C) £30.52 million

(D) £30.43 million

(E) £30 million

2   At an exchange rate of €1.20 to the £, what is the cost (in £) of three boxes of office paper at €6.60 per box?

(A) £12.50

(B) £14.50

(C) £16.50

(D) £18.50

(E) £23.76

3   A company profit and loss account contains the following operating costs: infrastructure (£2.1 million); transport (£2.8 million); and salaries (£7.7 million). What is the ratio between the operating costs for infrastructure, transport and salaries?

(A) 3:4:11

(B) 2.8:2.1:7.7

(C) None of these

(D) 28:77:21

(E) 7:8:1

4   Sales team A makes sales of £92,500, £69,000, £115,600 and £89,000 for Quarters 1–4, respectively. If there were 15 members in this team, what sales is each sales person making on average per month (to the nearest £)?

(A) £2,034

(B) £16,474

(C) £32,949

(D) £43,932

(E) £65,898

5   A broadband provider has two packages: one costs £24.00 per month, the other an extra £5.00 per month for a super-fast broadband option. What is the annual difference in cost between the two packages?

(A) No difference

(B) £40.00

(C) £50.00

(D) £60.00

(E) £70.00

6   The current year's UK earnings for an airline operator are predicted to be 15% less than last year's £4.85 million. The current year's US earnings are predicted to be 25% more than last year's £10.3 million. What is the difference in earnings predicted to be between the UK and US (to the nearest million)?

(A) £5 million

(B) £6 million

(C) £7 million

(D) £8 million

(E) £9 million

7   The market share of a leading CD retail chain is 28.4%. Its two main rivals have 14.2% and 10.8% of the market share, respectively. Given a total market size of €53 million, what is the value of the market outside these three retailers (to the nearest million euros)?

(A) 25

(B) 26

(C) 27

(D) 28

(E) 29

8   A world-wide tour operator has 3,500 employees. There is an average of 250 employees in each of the eight European countries where it operates. What fraction of employees work in Europe?

(A) ¹⁄₇

(B) ²⁄₇

(C) ³⁄₇

(D) ⁴⁄₇

(E) ⁵⁄₇

9   An IT consultancy company pays 8% of its total annual costs on rent and 74% on salaries. If its total annual costs are £620,000, what is the total of the other costs (excluding rent and salaries)?

(A) £49,600

(B) £99,200

(C) £111,600

(D) £229,400

(E) £458,800

10 The average salary of an electrician at a car manufacturer is £44,500 and is due to rise in line with inflation of 3% a year over the next 3 years. What is the electrician's average salary in 3 year's time?

(A) £45,835

(B) £47,626

(C) £48,505

(D) £48,626

(E) £48,835

Review your answers to practice test 2

1   **Answer (D) is correct: £30.43 million**
    $42.6 million/1.40 = £30.43 million

2   **Answer (C) is correct: £16.50**
    €6.60 × 3 = €19.80
    19.80/1.20 = 16.50

3   **Answer (A) is correct: 3:4:11**
    Infrastructure (£2.1 million): transport (£2.8 million):
    salaries (£7.7 million)
    2.1:2.8:7.7
    Dividing by 7 gives 3:4:11.

4   **Answer (A) is correct: £2,034**
    Total sales of team A = £92,500 + £69,000 + £115,600
    + £89,000 = £366,100
    Average per sales person = £366,100/15 = £24,407
    Average per sales person per month = £24,407/12 = £2,034

5   **Answer (D) is correct: £60.00**
    Package 1 = £24.00 × 12 = £288.00 a year
    Package 2 = (£24.00 + £5.00) × 12 = £348.00 a year
    Annual difference in cost between the two packages =
    £348.00 − £288.00 = £60.00

6   **Answer (E) is correct: £9 million**
    The current year's UK earnings for an airline operator are
    predicted to be 15% less than last year's.
    UK earnings: £4.85 million × 85/100 = £4.1225 million
    US earnings: £10.3 million × 125/100 = £12.875 million
    Difference in earnings predicted between the UK and US
    = £12.875 million − £4.1225 million = £8.7525 million
    To the nearest million: £8.7525 million = £9 million

7   **Answer (A) is correct: 25 (to the nearest million euros)**
    28.4% + 14.2% + 10.8% = 53.4%
    100% = €53 million

Value of the market outside these three retailers = 100% − 53.4% = 46.6%

46.6/100 × €53 million = €24.7 million

8   **Answer (D) is correct:** $^4/_7$

250 × 8 = 2,000

2,000/3,500 = $^4/_7$

9   **Answer (C) is correct: £111,600**

8% + 74% = 82% on rent and salary costs

Total annual costs = £620,000 = 100%

Total of other costs (excluding rent and salaries) = 18% of £620,000

£620,000 × 18/100 = £111,600

10   **Answer (D) is correct: £48,626**

Year 1 increase = £44,500 × 103/100 = £45,835

Year 2 increase = £45,835 × 103/100 = £47,210

Year 3 increase = £47,210 × 103/100 = £48,626

Numerical comprehension practice test 3

1   Demand for office rental property in an office block fell by
    a quarter during 2008. If it was 82% full at the start of 2008
    what was the percentage occupancy by the end of 2008?
    (A) 615%
    (B) 61.5%
    (C) 56%
    (D) 5.6%
    (E) 6.15%

2   A sales rep spends one-fifth of his time travelling and a
    third of his time meeting clients. In a typical 30-hour week
    how many hours approximately does this sales rep spend on
    other tasks (apart from travelling and meeting clients)?
    (A) 14
    (B) 12
    (C) 11
    (D) 9
    (E) 7

3   A consultancy's operating costs to turnover ratio is 3:20
    each year. If the company's turnover is £213,250 in Year
    1, £268,460 in Year 2 and £328,915 in Year 3 what are the
    total operating costs for the three-year period?
    (A) £121,594
    (B) £211,694
    (C) £328,915
    (D) £528,894
    (E) £810,625

4   An expenses budget of £640 is spread amongst seven teams,
    although one team gets twice as much as the others who
    each receive an equal amount. How much do the other six
    teams receive each?
    (A) Can't say
    (B) £60

(C) £70

(D) £80

(E) £90

5   Of the 42 staff employed by a market research company in
     a ratio of 2:1 at two sites, the workforce at the company's
     smaller site is to be cut by a half. What fraction of total staff
     does this reduction represent?

     (A) ⅑

     (B) ⅛

     (C) ⅐

     (D) ⅙

     (E) ⅕

6   Advertising spend by a utility company is predicted to grow by
     £125,000 a year. If the current advertising spend is £725,000
     then what will the advertising spend be in five year's time?

     (A) £125,000

     (B) £135,000

     (C) £1,250,000

     (D) £1,350,000

     (E) £1,400,000

7   The carbon dioxide emission rate for the average car is 145
     g/km. How much carbon dioxide (to the nearest kg) would
     be emitted over a 145 km journey?

     (A) 21 kg

     (B) 19 kg

     (C) 17 kg

     (D) 15 kg

     (E) 12 kg

8   The market for online advertising in the UK is estimated
     to be worth £3.2 billion. The error band for this is 1/20th
     higher and 1/20th lower. What are the lower and higher esti-
     mates of the online advertising market?

     (A) £3.02 billion–£3.34 billion

(B) £3.04 billion–£3.36 billion

(C) £3.06 billion–£3.38 billion

(D) £3.08 billion–£3.40 billion

(E) £3.10 billion–£3.42 billion

9   A company's value increased by 4% in Year 1, by 5% in Year 2 and by 4.5% in Year 3. If the company was valued at £2.15 million at the start of Year 1 then what is its value at the end of Year 3?

(A) £2.41 million

(B) £2.44 million

(C) £2.45 million

(D) £24.1 million

(E) £24.5 million

10   The total cost of a litre of milk is 24.5p. What is the profit (to the nearest £) on 2,500 gallons of milk that is sold in two-litre cartons for £1.05 (1 gallon = 4.546 litres)?

(A) £5,967

(B) £3,182

(C) £2,784

(D) £597

(E) £318

Review your answers to practice test 3

1   **Answer (B) is correct: 61.5%**
$82\% \times {}^3\!/_4 = 61.5\%$

2   **Answer (A) is correct: 14**
$^1\!/_5 + {}^1\!/_3 = {}^3\!/_{15} + {}^5\!/_{15} = {}^8\!/_{15}$
$1 - {}^8\!/_{15} = {}^7\!/_{15}$
$^7\!/_{15} \times 30\text{-hour week} = 14 \text{ hours}$

3   **Answer (A) is correct: £121,594**
Total costs = £213,250 + £268,460 + £328,915 = £810,625
Operating costs = $3/20 \times £810,625 = £121,593.75$

4   **Answer (D) is correct: £80**
Let x = amount that each team gets:
$2x + 6x = 640$
$x = 640/8 = 80$

5   **Answer (D) is correct: $^1\!/_6$**
42 staff in a 2:1 ratio means that 14 staff work at one site and 28 staff at the other site. So, cutting the workforce at the company's smaller site by 50% = seven staff:
$^7\!/_{42} = {}^1\!/_6$

6   **Answer (D) is correct: £1,350,000**
£725,000 + (5 × £125,000) = £1,350,000

7   **Answer (A) is correct: 21 kg to the nearest kg**
$145 \times 145 \text{ g} = 21,025 \text{ g}$
$1,000 \text{ g} = 1 \text{ kg}$
So 21,025 g = 21,025 kg

8   **Answer (B) is correct: £3.04 billion–£3.36 billion**
£3.2 billion × 95/100 = £3.04 billion
£3.2 billion × 105/100 = £3.36 billion

9   **Answer (C) is correct: £2.45 million**

This requires you to work out cumulative interest:

£2.15 million × 104/100 = £2.23 million

£2.23 million × 105/100 = £2.34 million

£2.34 million × 104.5/100 = £2.45 million

10 **Answer (B) is correct: £3,182 (to the nearest £)**

Note firstly that profit = total sales – total cost.

Note secondly that the calculation needs to be in litres throughout.

Milk quantity sold (in litres) = 2,500 gallons × 4.546/2

So, total sales (of 2,500 gallons of milk) = £1.05 × (2,500 × 4.546/2) = £5,966.63

Total cost (using litres of milk) = 24.5p × 2,500 × 4.546 = £2,784.43

Profit = total sales – total cost = £5,966.63 – £2,784.43 = £3,182.20

CHAPTER 7

Warm-up numerical reasoning tests

Introduction to this format

This chapter's numerical reasoning questions are described as an intermediary, warm-up type of question. In comparison with the previous chapter there is, once again, a slight increase in difficulty alongside an increase in the complexity of the question format.

The chapter introduces the most commonly used type of numerical reasoning test: a table of data followed by questions asking you to extract and interpret the figures given. You might be given line graphs, bar charts, pie charts – any format that can appear in business or professional reports. It is worth thinking about the types of tables and graphs that you would encounter in a business context: sales figures, attendance figures, costs, budgets, and such like. That's exactly the sort of thing that appears in these tests.

brilliant example – RAF's Airman Selection Test (AST)

Applying to the RAF is a process that takes several months from initial application through to acceptance. The staged selection process involves interviews, a fitness test and, of course, aptitude tests. The tests that you are asked to take will depend upon the particular RAF career that you are applying for: officer, non-commissioned aircrew or airman/airwoman. This practice test aims to prepare you for the numerical reasoning components of the Airman Selection Test (AST).

The RAF's AST is used as part of the process for becoming an airman/airwoman. The AST comprises the following seven multiple choice tests: verbal reasoning; numerical reasoning; work rate; spatial reasoning; electrical comprehension; mechanical comprehension; and memory.

The numerical reasoning portion of the AST is in two parts. The first part assesses your ability to use fractions and decimals. You are given four minutes to answer 12 questions. The second part assesses your ability to interpret graphs and tables. There are 15 questions to answer in 11 minutes.

Guidance for warm-up numerical reasoning tests

For ease of use, this chapter's practice questions have been grouped into sets of five questions. Answering all five questions and then reviewing your answers will help to keep you engaged during your practice sessions. Completing all the test questions should highlight to you the types of questions that you find easy and those that, for the time being, are more difficult. Focus your practice on the latter type of questions so as to improve your overall performance.

You are advised to:

● allow yourself 10 minutes to complete each set of 5 questions;

● read each question carefully – twice if necessary;

● choose the correct answer from the multiple-choice options shown;

● check your answers against the answer explanations that follow the test once you have completed all 5 questions;

- do this before you move on to the next test so that you can apply anything you have learnt immediately – this will aid your memory;
- use a calculator to answer the questions.

brilliant tips

- Focus and concentration are key when adopting the necessary engaged approach that you will need when taking your test for real. Use these practice tests to practise getting your mind into that 'zone'.

- Try to make your practice sessions as realistic as possible. That means making your home environment as quiet and as free as possible from the usual distractions (Internet, mobile phone, etc.).

- A time estimate has been given for each test to focus your practice and to allow you to work under realistic, timed conditions.

Warm-up numerical reasoning practice test 1

Food product price increases

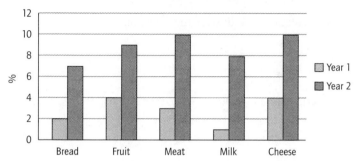

1   Which food product increased by the smallest % in Year 1?
    (A) Bread
    (B) Fruit
    (C) Meat
    (D) Milk
    (E) Cheese

2   The average cost of bread at the start of Year 1 is £1.10.
    What is the average cost of bread at the end of Year 1?
    (A) £1.10
    (B) £1.11
    (C) £1.12
    (D) £1.13
    (E) £1.14

3   Which food products increased by more than 8% in Year 2?
    (A) Bread, fruit and cheese
    (B) Fruit, meat and cheese
    (C) Fruit, meat, milk and cheese
    (D) Meat, milk and cheese
    (E) Meat and cheese

4   Which two food products increased by 4% in Year 1?
    (A) Bread and cheese

(B) Meat and cheese

(C) Fruit and meat

(D) Meat and milk

(E) Fruit and cheese

5   The average cost of cheese at the end of Year 2 is £2.75. What was the average cost at the end of Year 1?

(A) £2.50

(B) £2.55

(C) £2.60

(D) £2.65

(E) £2.70

Review your answers to practice test 1

1 **Answer (D) is correct: Milk**

2 **Answer (C) is correct: £1.12**

3 **Answer (B) is correct: Fruit, meat and cheese**

4 **Answer (E) is correct: Fruit and cheese**

5 **Answer (A) is correct: £2.50**

Warm-up numerical reasoning practice test 2

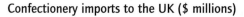

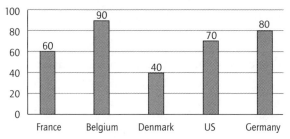

Confectionery imports to the UK ($ millions)

1   Which countries have the highest and the lowest confectionery exports to the UK?
    (A) France and Belgium
    (B) Belgium and Denmark
    (C) Germany and Denmark
    (D) Belgium and France
    (E) Germany and Belgium

2   From which countries is the level of confectionery imports more than 20% higher than the French level?
    (A) US and Belgium
    (B) Belgium, US and Germany
    (C) Belgium
    (D) US and Germany
    (E) Belgium and Germany

3   The level of confectionery imports from Denmark increases by a quarter. What is the new amount (£ millions)?
    (A) 42
    (B) 45
    (C) 48
    (D) 50
    (E) 60

4   What is the total amount of confectionery imports across the five countries (£ millions)?

(A) 300

(B) 320

(C) 340

(D) 360

(E) 380

5   The amount of confectionery imports from the US doubled in the following year. What is the new level of confectionery imports from the US (£ millions)?

(A) 120

(B) 125

(C) 130

(D) 135

(E) 140

Review your answers to practice test 2

1   **Answer (B) is correct: Belgium and Denmark**

2   **Answer (E) is correct: Belgium and Germany**

3   **Answer (D) is correct: 50**

4   **Answer (C) is correct: 340**

5   **Answer (E) is correct: 140**

Warm-up numerical reasoning practice test 3

	2 nights	4 nights
St Ives – Kings Hotel	£140	£229
Eastbourne – Prior Hotel	£95	£175
Newquay – Major Hotel	£120	£215
Brighton – Bains Hotel	£110	£189
Bexhill – Eddy's Hotel	£99	£165
Brighton – Dune Roaming Hotel	£115	£205

1   A surfer is planning a holiday that takes in two nights at the Major Hotel in Newquay and four nights at the Kings Hotel in St Ives. What would the total cost be?
   (A) £290
   (B) £315
   (C) £349
   (D) £355
   (E) £369

2   A couple is planning to spend four nights at Eastbourne (Prior Hotel). What is the total cost of their stay?
   (A) £165
   (B) £175
   (C) £215
   (D) £229
   (E) £350

3   A father plans to stay with his son – who pays half price – for two nights at Newquay (Major Hotel). What is the total cost of their stay?
   (A) £150
   (B) £160
   (C) £170
   (D) £180
   (E) £190

4   Which hotels are the cheapest for two and for four nights?
    (A) St Ives (Kings Hotel) and Bexhill (Eddy's Hotel)
    (B) Eastbourne (Prior Hotel) and Brighton (Bains Hotel)
    (C) Newquay (Major Hotel) and Brighton (Bains Hotel)
    (D) Eastbourne (Prior Hotel) and Bexhill (Eddy's Hotel)
    (E) Brighton (Dune Roaming Hotel) and St Ives (Kings
        Hotel)

5   Brighton (Bains Hotel) starts a promotion offering a 20%
    reduction for a two night stay. What is the new cost of a two
    night stay?
    (A) £88
    (B) £90
    (C) £98
    (D) £100
    (E) £108

Review your answers to practice test 3

1   **Answer (C) is correct: £349**

2   **Answer (B) is correct: £175**

3   **Answer (D) is correct: £180**

4   **Answer (D) is correct: Eastbourne (Prior Hotel) and Bexhill (Eddy's Hotel)**

5   **Answer (A) is correct: £88**

Warm-up numerical reasoning practice test 4

Location	Minimum temperature (degrees Celsius)	Maximum temperature (degrees Celsius)	Maximum temperature (degrees Fahrenheit)
Lisbon	15	24	75
Madrid	12	25	77
Athens	22	28	82
London	13	15	59
Cardiff	14	17	63

1   Which two cities have the highest and the lowest temperatures?
   (A) Athens and Cardiff
   (B) Lisbon and Madrid
   (C) Athens and Madrid
   (D) Lisbon and Cardiff
   (E) Lisbon and London

2   Which city has the greatest difference between the minimum and the maximum temperatures?
   (A) Lisbon
   (B) Madrid
   (C) Athens
   (D) London
   (E) Cardiff

3   What is the range of maximum temperatures across the cities shown (in degrees Fahrenheit)?
   (A) 59–82
   (B) 63–82
   (C) 17–28
   (D) 15–25
   (E) 15–28

4   Which city has the highest maximum temperature (in degrees Fahrenheit)?
   (A) Lisbon

(B) Madrid

(C) Athens

(D) London

(E) Cardiff

5   Which two cities have maximum temperatures below 20 degrees Celsius?

(A) Athens and Cardiff

(B) Lisbon and Madrid

(C) Athens and Madrid

(D) Madrid and Cardiff

(E) London and Cardiff

Review your answers to practice test 4

1   **Answer (C) is correct: Athens and Madrid**

2   **Answer (B) is correct: Madrid**

3   **Answer (A) is correct: 59–82**

4   **Answer (C) is correct: Athens**

5   **Answer (E) is correct: London and Cardiff**

Warm-up numerical reasoning practice test 5

Coal demand (million tonnes)

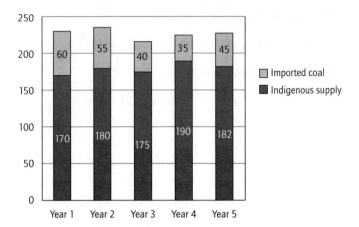

1   What has been the average amount of imported coal over the five years shown?
    (A) 40 million tonnes
    (B) 44 million tonnes
    (C) 47 million tonnes
    (D) 50 million tonnes
    (E) 54 million tonnes

2   In which year was the coal demand met from imported coal the lowest relative to that met from indigenous sources?
    (A) Year 1
    (B) Year 2
    (C) Year 3
    (D) Year 4
    (E) Year 5

3   The total coal demand for each year is the sum of the imported and indigenous supply figures. Put the total coal demand for each year in size order, starting with the highest.
    (A) Year 2, Year 1, Year 5, Year 4, Year 3

(B) Year 2, Year 1, Year 4, Year 5, Year 3

(C) Year 2, Year 1, Year 4, Year 3, Year 5

(D) Year 2, Year 5, Year 1, Year 4, Year 3

(E) Year 2, Year 5, Year 1, Year 3, Year 4

4   Between which years was there the greatest proportional change in the coal demand from indigenous supplies?

(A) Years 1–2

(B) Years 2–3

(C) Years 3–4

(D) Years 4–5

(E) Can't tell

5   In which year or years was the ratio of imported coal to indigenous source coal less than 1:4?

(A) Year 1

(B) Year 2

(C) Year 1 and Year 2

(D) Year 3 and Year 5

(E) Year 3, Year 4 and Year 5

Review your answers to practice test 5

1   **Answer (C) is correct: 47 million tonnes**
    Average amount of imported coal over the five years shown
    = (60 + 55 + 40 + 35 + 45)/5 = 235/5 = 47

2   **Answer (D) is correct: Year 4**
    Divide the imported coal by the indigenous coal for each
    year:
    (A) Year 1 = 60/170 = 0.35
    (B) Year 2 = 55/180 = 0.31
    (C) Year 3 = 40/175 = 0.23
    (D) Year 4 = 35/190 = 0.18
    (E) Year 5 = 45/182 = 0.25

3   **Answer (A) is correct: Year 2, Year 1, Year 5, Year 4,
    Year 3**
    Year 2 is clearly the highest and Year 3 the lowest. Then,
    calculate the totals to rank order the other three years (Years
    1, 4 and 5):
    Year 1 = 230 million tonnes
    Year 4 = 225 million tonnes
    Year 5 = 227 million tonnes
    Putting these years in order of decreasing total coal demand:
    Year 2, Year 1, Year 5, Year 4, Year 3

4   **Answer (C) is correct: Years 3–4**

brilliant tip

Question 4 could be answered without doing the actual
calculations; it is clear that the largest change in indigenous supply
is the increase from 175 to 190 million tonnes between Year 3 and
Year 4.

5   **Answer (E) is correct: Year 3, Year 4 and Year 5**
Step 1: For the ratio of imported coal to indigenous source
coal to be less than 1:4 there needs to be more than four times
the amount of indigenous coal compared to imported coal.

Step 2: Review the coal demand figures given in the graph.
There are three years when the amount of indigenous coal
compared to imported coal is more than four times greater.

Answer A is incorrect: the ratio is 60:170 or 2.83
Answer B is incorrect: the ratio is 55:180 or 3.27
Answer C is incorrect therefore
Answer D is incorrect: the ratios are 4.375 and 4.044 but
there could be another year also
Answer E is correct: the ratios of these three years are all
greater than 4

Numerical reasoning practice test 6

The table shows the peak cost of a week's stay in three resorts situated in the South of France. Children under 16 years of age are charged at 60% of the price quoted.

	St Michaels (£)	St John (£)	Bellevue (£)
July	910	950	999
August	845	870	929
September	789	810	855

1 Which is the cheapest and most expensive holiday resort and month?
   (A) St Michaels – August (cheapest), St John – July (most expensive)
   (B) St John – September (cheapest), Bellevue – July (most expensive)
   (C) St John – September (cheapest), St Michaels – July (most expensive)
   (D) St Michaels – September (cheapest), Bellevue – July (most expensive)
   (E) Bellevue – September (cheapest), St Michaels – July (most expensive)

2 What is the price difference for two people between a week's holiday in August staying at St Michaels compared to the St John resort?
   (A) £35.00
   (B) £25.00
   (C) £75.00
   (D) £84.00
   (E) £50.00

3 There is a reduction of 5% for booking online. What is the cost difference of booking a two-week holiday online at

Bellevue in September, compared to an offline, two-week booking at St Michaels?

(A) £46.50

(B) £132.00

(C) £66.00

(D) £66.50

(E) £112.50

4   What would the cost difference be for a couple going to St John on a week's holiday in August compared to parents with a young child booking the same holiday?

(A) £780.00

(B) £1,740.00

(C) £522.00

(D) £870.00

(E) £348.00

5   The holiday company refunds 50% of a holiday that is cancelled with one week's notice. What refund would a group of four people receive who had booked a week's holiday in September at St Michaels?

(A) £1,578.00

(B) None of these

(C) £789.00

(D) £394.50

(E) £3,156.00

Review your answers to practice test 6

1 **Answer (D) is correct: St Michaels – September (cheapest), Bellevue – July (most expensive)**
Review the nine pieces of data supplied in the table. Which is the highest, i.e. the most expensive? Which is the lowest, i.e. the cheapest?

2 **Answer (E) is correct: £50.00**
Step 1: Find the figure in the data table for the cost of a week's holiday for two people in August at St Michaels:
$2 \times £845 = £1,690$

Step 2: Find the figure in the data table for the cost of a week's holiday for two people in August at the St John resort:
$2 \times £870 = £1,740$

Step 3: Find the difference between the *Step 1* and *Step 2* results:
$£1,740 - £1,690 = £50.00$

3 **Answer (A) is correct: £46.50**
Step 1: Calculate the cost of a two-week holiday online at Bellevue in September, compared to an offline, two-week booking at St Michaels
$(2 \times £855) \times 95\% = £1,624.50$

Step 2: Calculate the cost of an offline, two-week booking at St Michaels:
$2 \times £789 = £1,578$

Step 3: Find the cost difference:
$£1,624.50 - £1,578 = £46.50$

4 **Answer (C) is correct: £522**
Calculate the cost for a young child going to St John on a week's holiday in August. *You can ignore the rest of the question*

as the cost for the two couples is the same, the only difference being the additional cost for the child.

£870 × 60% = £522

5   **Answer (A) is correct: £1,578**

Step 1: Calculate the cost of the holiday for a group of four people staying for a week in September at St Michaels:

4 × £789 = £3,156

Step 2: Calculate the refunds at a rate of 50%:

£3,156 × 50% = £1,578

Numerical reasoning practice test 7

Sales by market region	Quarter 1 (£100,000s)	Quarter 2 (£100,000s)	Quarter 3 (£100,000s)	Quarter 4 (£100,000s)
UK	58.19	34.21	32.91	32.90
US	62.23	16.14	16.81	16.89
Far East	41.34	46.60	46.67	46.76
Other markets	9.42	6.73	5.24	5.24

1   What were the total sales across Quarters 1 and 2 (in £100,000s)?
   (A) 478.55
   (B) None of these
   (C) 274.86
   (D) 171.18
   (E) 103.95

2   Which market region has experienced an increase in sales each quarter?
   (A) Other markets
   (B) None of these
   (C) UK
   (D) US
   (E) Far East

3   At an exchange rate of $1.62 to the £, what is the total US sales value (in $100,000s) for all four quarters?
   (A) $18
   (B) $182
   (C) $158
   (D) $256
   (E) $112

4   What is the absolute change in Far East sales when compared to the previous year's Quarter 3 sales of £4,550,000?
   (A) £121,500 decrease
   (B) £117,000 decrease

(C) £117,000 increase

(D) £126,000 decrease

(E) £126,000 increase

5   Which market region has shown a 42% change in value between Quarters 1 and 4?

(A) UK

(B) US

(C) Far East

(D) Other markets

(E) None of these

Review your answers to practice test 7

1   **Answer (C) is correct: 274.86**
Step 1: Sum the four regional sales figures for Quarter 1:
$58.19 + 62.23 + 41.34 + 9.42 = 171.18$

Step 2: Sum the four regional sales figures for Quarter 2:
$34.21 + 16.14 + 46.60 + 6.73 = 103.68$

Step 3: Add the *Step 1* and *Step 2* answers together:
$171.18 + 103.68 = 274.86$

2   **Answer (E) is correct: Far East**
Review the four market regions to determine which one has increased its sales figure between Quarters 1 and 2, Quarters 2 and 3 and Quarters 3 and 4.

3   **Answer (B) is correct: $182**
Step 1: Sum the US sales revenue for all four quarters:
$62.23 + 16.14 + 16.81 + 16.89 = 112.07$

Step 2: Convert from £100,000 into $100,000 (at an exchange rate of $1.62 to the £):
$112.07 \times 1.62 = 181.55$

Step 3: To the nearest $100,000:
$181.55 = 182$

4   **Answer (C) is correct: £117,000 increase**
Calculate the difference between Far East Quarter 3 sales and the previous year's:
£4,667,000 − £4,550,000 = £117,000 increase

5   **Answer (E) is correct: None of these**
Calculate the percentage change for each region:
UK: $100\% \times (58.19 - 32.9)/58.19 = 43.5\%$
US: $100\% \times (62.23 - 16.89)/62.23 = 72.9\%$
Far East: $100\% \times (41.34 - 46.76)/41.34 = 12.4\%$
Other markets: $100\% \times (9.42 - 5.24)/9.42 = 44.4\%$

Warm-up numerical reasoning practice test 8

Costs for Company X	2012 (£10,000s)	2013 (£10,000s)	2014 (£10,000s)
Premises	15.24	15.45	14.97
Staff salaries	174.77	163.50	172.95
Marketing	6.85	6.29	7.64
IT	5.24	4.78	3.37
Misc costs	4.19	5.25	6.34

1   If there were 49 Company X employees in 2013 what was the average salary per employee?
   (A) £43,367
   (B) £53,367
   (C) £33,367
   (D) £13,367
   (E) £23,367

2   Which Company X cost has decreased in value each year?
   (A) IT
   (B) Premises
   (C) Misc costs
   (D) Marketing
   (E) Staff salaries

3   What is the difference in total costs between 2012 and 2014?
   (A) £10,000
   (B) £10,200
   (C) £20,000
   (D) £20,100
   (E) £20,500

4   What were the total costs for 2012?
   (A) £0.21 million
   (B) £21 million
   (C) £20.6 million

(D) £1.95 million

(E) £2.06 million

5   What was the increase in Marketing and Misc costs between 2012 and 2014?

(A) £29,000

(B) £29,100

(C) £29,200

(D) £29,300

(E) £29,400

Review your answers to practice test 8

1   **Answer (C) is correct: £33,367**
    Step 1: Find the **Staff salaries** figure for 2013 in the table:
    163.50 (£10,000s)

    Step 2: Find the average: total/number = 1,635,000/49 = £33,367

2   **Answer (A) is correct: IT**
    Reviewing the data table, which of the five costs have decreased between 2012 and 2013 and between 2013 and 2014?

    Answer A (**IT**) is correct
    Answer B (**Premises**) is incorrect
    Answer C (**Misc costs**) is incorrect
    Answer D (**Marketing**) is incorrect
    Answer E (**Staff salaries**) is incorrect

3   **Answer (B) is correct: £10,200**
    Step 1: Sum the five individual costs for 2012:
    15.24 + 174.77 + 6.85 + 5.24 + 4.19 = 206.29

    Step 2: Sum the five individual costs for 2014:
    14.97 + 172.95 + 7.64 + 3.37 + 6.34 = 205.27

    Step 3: Calculate the difference between the *Step 1* and *Step 2* answers:
    206.29 − 205.27 = 1.02 (£10,000) = £10,200

4   **Answer (E) is correct: £2.06 million**
    Step 1: Sum the five individual costs for 2012:
    15.24 + 174.77+ 6.85+ 5.24+ 4.19 = 206.29

    Step 2: Convert from £10,000s:
    206.29 in £10,000s = 2,062,900 = £2.06 million

5   **Answer (E) is correct: £29,400**
    Step 1: Find the total Marketing and Misc costs in 2012:
    6.85 + 4.19 = 11.04

Step 2: Find the total Marketing and Misc costs in 2014:
7.64 + 6.34 = 13.98

Step 3: Find the difference:
13.98 − 11.04 = (£10,000s) = £29,400

Numerical reasoning practice test 9

Viewers (1,000s)	Channel A	Channel B
January	4.1	4.3
February	4.2	4.8
March	4.3	4.5
April	4.7	4.3
May	4.2	4.9
June	4.6	4.8

1   In which months were there over 300 more viewers of Channel B than Channel A?

(A) May

(B) February and May

(C) March and May

(D) February

(E) February, May and June

2   In which month were there more viewers of Channel A than Channel B?

(A) March

(B) January

(C) April

(D) February

(E) May

3   If in February 50% of Channel A viewers had switched to Channel B what would be Channel B's viewer numbers?

(A) 6,700

(B) 6,800

(C) 6,900

(D) 7,000

(E) 7,100

4   In which month was there the highest number of Channel A and Channel B viewers?

(A) January

(B) March
(C) April
(D) May
(E) June

5   For which two months were there as many combined Channel A and Channel B viewers?
(A) May and April
(B) May and June
(C) April and June
(D) February and April
(E) February and March

Review your answers to practice test 9

1   **Answer (B) is correct: February and May**
    Find the monthly difference in Channel B viewers compared to Channel A viewers:
    Jan: 4.3 − 4.1=200 more
    Feb: 4.8 − 4.2=600 more
    March: 4.5 − 4.3=200 more
    April: 4.3 − 4.7=400 less
    May: 4.9 − 4.2=700 more
    June: 4.8 − 4.6 = 200 more
    Answer A is correct: **May**. However, as the table shows, there is another month too (February)
    Answer B is correct: **February and May**
    Answer C is incorrect: **March and May** since March is incorrect
    Answer D is incorrect: **February**
    Answer E is incorrect: **February, May and June** since February is incorrect

2   **Answer (C) is correct: April**
    The calculation for Question 1 will also provide the answer for Question 2. There is only one month during which there were more viewers of Channel A than Channel B.

3   **Answer (C) is correct: 6,900**
    Step 1: Find 50% of 4.2:
    $4.2 \times 50/100 = 2.1$

    Step 2: Find the absolute number of Channel B viewers:
    $4.8 + 2.1 = 6.9$

    Step 3: Convert 6.9 (1,000s) = 6,900:

4   **Answer (E) is correct: June**
    Total the number of Channel A and Channel B viewers for each month:
    Jan: 4.1 + 4.3 = 8.4

Feb: 4.2 + 4.8 = 9.0
March: 4.3 + 4.5 = 8.8
April: 4.7 + 4.3 = 9.0
May: 4.2 + 4.9 = 9.1
June: 4.6 + 4.8 = 9.4

5   **Answer (D) is correct: February and April**
Referring to the sums in the previous question, the two months must be February and April.

Numerical reasoning practice test 10

	Product A (£10,000s)	Product B (£10,000s)	Product C (£10,000s)	Product D (£10,000s)
Marketing spend	27.5	20.0	22.5	20.0
Marketing budget	30.0	25.0	20.0	17.5

1   If the exchange rate is €1.05 to the £ then what is the discrepancy between the marketing spend and budget for Product C in euros?
   (A) €2,500
   (B) €26,250
   (C) €22,500
   (D) €27,000
   (E) €25,000

2   Compared to the previous year's figure, the total marketing spend has increased by 20%. What was the previous year's total marketing spend?
   (A) £710,000
   (B) £720,000
   (C) £730,000
   (D) £740,000
   (E) £750,000

3   Next year's marketing budget for Products A, B, C and D is going to be cut by a fifth. What is next year's marketing budget (in €10,000s)? Use an exchange rate of €1.05 to the £ and give your answer to the nearest €10,000.
   (A) 74
   (B) 76
   (C) 78
   (D) 80
   (E) 82

4   For which two products was there the same overspend when compared to budget?

(A) Products A and C

(B) Products B and C

(C) Products A and D

(D) Products B and D

(E) Products C and D

5   What is the total difference between Marketing budget and Marketing spend?

(A) £2,500 overspend

(B) £250,000 overspend

(C) £2,500 underspend

(D) £25,000 overspend

(E) £25,000 underspend

Review your answers to practice test 10

1 **Answer (B) is correct: £26,250**
Step 1: Calculate the discrepancy between Marketing spend and Marketing budget for Product C:
22.5 − 20 = 2.5 (£25,000)

Step 2: Convert to euros (given the exchange rate in the question):
£25,000 × 1.05 = €26,250

2 **Answer (E) is correct: £750,000**
Step 1: Calculate the total Marketing spend:
27.5 + 20 + 22.5 + 20 = 90

Step 2: This year's figure for total Marketing spend is 120% of last year's. Therefore, last year's figure (100%) is:
90/120 × 100 = 75 (£10,000s) = £750,000

3 **Answer (C) is correct: 78**
Step 1: Calculate the total Marketing budget by summing the Marketing budgets for Products A, B, C and D:
30 + 25 + 20 + 17.5 = 92.5

Step 2 Option (a): Calculate ⅕ of the total Marketing budget and deduct this amount from the *Step 1* answer:
92.5 × ⅕ = 18.5
92.5 − 18.5 = 74 (£10,000s) = £740,000

Step 2 Option (b): A quicker calculation – since it has one less stage – is to calculate ⅘ of the total Marketing budget:
⅘ × 92.5 = £740,000

Step 3: Convert to euros (the exchange rate is €1.05 to the £):
£740,000 × €1.05 = €770,700

Step 4: Give your answer to the nearest €10,000:
78

4   **Answer (D) is correct: Products C and D**
Step 1: Calculate the difference between Marketing budget and Marketing spend for each product:

$30 - 27.5 = 2.5$ Product A
$25 - 20 = 5$ Product B
$20 - 22.5 = -2.5$ Product C
$17.5 - 20 = -2.5$ Product D

Step 2: Review the above to find which two products have the same overspend:
Products C and D

5   **Answer (E) is correct: £25,000 underspend**
Step 1: Calculate the total Marketing spend by adding Products A, B, C and D's Marketing spend
(or refer back to your answer to *Step 1* in Question 2):
$27.5 + 20 + 22.5 + 20 = 90$

Step 2: Calculate the total Marketing budget by adding Products A, B, C and D's Marketing budget
(or refer back to your answer to *Step 1* in Question 3):
$30 + 25 + 20 + 17.5 = 92.5$

Step 3: Find the difference between *Step 1* and *Step 2*:
$92.5 - 90 = 2.5$ (£10,000s) $=$ £25,000 underspend

Warm-up numerical reasoning practice test 11

Office paper supply and demand (tonnes)

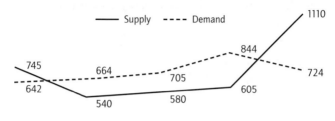

Month 1   Month 2   Month 3   Month 4   Month 5

1   In which month(s) was the office paper demand the most in
    excess of the office paper supply?
    (A) Month 1
    (B) Months 1 and 2
    (C) Months 2 and 3
    (D) Month 4
    (E) Month 5

2   Over the five-month period what is the total difference
    between supply and demand?
    (A) 1 tonne
    (B) 2 tonnes
    (C) 3 tonnes
    (D) 4 tonnes
    (E) 5 tonnes

3   In which month was there a 103 tonnes difference in supply
    and demand?
    (A) Month 1
    (B) Month 2
    (C) Month 3

(D) Month 4

(E) Month 5

4   For how many months does supply exceed demand?

(A) 1 month

(B) 2 months

(C) 3 months

(D) 4 months

(E) 5 months

5   In which month was the demand for office paper 23% higher than the supply?

(A) Month 1

(B) Month 2

(C) Month 3

(D) Month 4

(E) Month 5

Review your answers to practice test 11

1   **The correct answer is (D): Month 4**
    Looking at the line graph you can see that there are three months when office paper demand is higher than supply:

    Month 4 clearly has the largest gap between the two lines on the graph (the difference = 844 − 605 although you may not need to work this out).

2   **The correct answer is (A): 1 tonne**
    Total difference between supply and demand = total supply − total demand = 3,580 − 3,579 = 1

3   **The correct answer is (A): Month 1**
    Starting with the first month, calculating the difference between supply and demand gives you the answer straight away:

    745 − 642 = 103 tonnes

4   **The correct answer is (B): 2 months**

5   **The correct answer is (B): Month 2**
    Step 1: Two of the answer options (Months 1 and 5) can be eliminated since supply exceeded demand in those months.

    Step 2: Calculate how much higher (in % terms) the demand is for Months 2, 3 and 4:
    Month 2: 100% × (664 − 540)/540 = 23.0%
    Month 3: 100% × (705 − 580)/580 = 21.6%
    Month 4: 100% × (844 − 605)/605 = 39.5%

CHAPTER 8

Numerical critical reasoning tests

Introduction to this format

The numerical reasoning format presented in Chapters 6 and 7 can vary quite considerably in difficulty level, and the questions in this chapter represent a further advance in numerical complexity. These questions are typical of those found in the UKCAT test for applicants to UK medical and dental schools, so if you are contemplating taking this test, these are the questions you need to practise.

The standard expected to pass such numerical reasoning tests as the UKCAT is a good Maths GCSE pass. The standard required for passing graduate tests starts around this level but – given the wide range of ability of today's graduates – the level stretches into the Advanced Data Interpretation Tests given in the final chapter. So, if you want additional practice and are up for the challenge, try these more difficult questions in Chapters 9 and 10.

---

brilliant example – UKCAT test for doctor training

Applicants to most British medical and dental schools will need to take the UKCAT. Healthcare workers must be able to work accurately with mathematical problems. The test enables universities to select the most suitable candidates from a large pool of talented applicants. Rather than focusing on academic achievements, the UKCAT tests the general mental abilities needed to be a successful healthcare professional.

▶

The UKCAT's difficulty level is set so as to sift graduates into those with the necessary numerical skills to pass their medical training. Many other graduate training schemes have more difficult numerical reasoning tests - as covered in subsequent chapters. For example, in training to become an accountant or learning how to become a banker a higher level of numerical reasoning is probably required.

Also, the more popular graduate recruitment schemes use the refined sift of a difficult numerical reasoning test as part of their benchmark for top graduates. When used in combination with a difficult verbal reasoning test and even an abstract reasoning test, the data interpretation tests that follow help the most popular graduate recruiters to select only the very best applicants for the next stage of the application process.

That said, the UKCAT is is not an academic test, but a test of your numerical reasoning rather than your ability to carry out a maths calculation. The UKCAT Consortium of Medical and Dental Schools and Pearson VUE run the UKCAT test process. You attend one of Pearson VUE's testing centres to take five multiple-choice subtests: Verbal Reasoning; Quantitative Reasoning; Abstract Reasoning; Decision Analysis; and Non-cognitive Analysis.

The Pearson VUE website (www.pearsonvue.co.uk) contains a lot of useful information on the UKCAT tests, including a case study and details on how the testing process is managed. You can find further practice questions and answer explanations at: www.ukcat.ac.uk

Guidance for these more difficult numerical reasoning tests

For ease of use, this chapter's practice questions have been grouped into sets of 5 questions. Answering all 5 questions and then reviewing your answers will help to keep you engaged during your practice sessions. Completing all the test questions should highlight to you the type of questions that you find easy and those that for the time being are more difficult. Focus your practice on the latter type of questions so as to improve your overall performance.

You are advised to:

- allow yourself 10 minutes to complete each set of 5 questions;

- read each question carefully – twice if necessary;

- choose the correct answer from the multiple-choice options shown;

- check your answers against the answer explanations that follow the test once you have completed all 5 questions;

- do this before you move on to the next test so that you can apply anything you have learnt immediately – this will aid your memory;

- use a calculator to answer the questions.

brilliant tips

- Keep the average of 'a minute and a half' in mind per question. Thus, if after doing a few questions each is taking you ...

  - more time, then you will need to speed up for the remaining questions

  - less time, then you are doing fine

- If you cannot decide upon an answer then try to eliminate some answer options and indicate which you think could be the correct answer.

Remember that you will get the most useful information from the questions you get wrong. So ensure that you fully understand each answer explanation before moving on to try more questions.

Numerical critical reasoning practice test 1

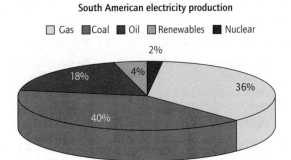

South American electricity production

☐ Gas ▨ Coal ■ Oil ▨ Renewables ■ Nuclear

1   What is the ratio of electricity generated from renewable sources to gas?
    (A) 1:7
    (B) 2:7
    (C) 1:9
    (D) 2:9
    (E) 1:11

2   What is the ratio of oil production to coal production expressed as a fraction?
    (A) $^9/_{20}$
    (B) $^{18}/_{40}$
    (C) $^1/_8$
    (D) $^1/_4$
    (E) $^1/_2$

3   South American electricity production is 55 GWh. How much is generated by nuclear power?
    (A) 5.5 GWh
    (B) 4.4 GWh
    (C) 3.3 GWh
    (D) 2.2 GWh
    (E) 1.1 GWh

4   South American electricity production is 700 GWh. What is
     the ratio of electricity generated by coal to gas and renew-
     able sources combined?
     (A) 1:1
     (B) 2:1
     (C) 1:2
     (D) 2:3
     (E) 1:3

5   South American electricity production is 500 GWh. What
     fraction of the total is generated by coal?
     (A) ⅔
     (B) ½
     (C) ⅖
     (D) ⅔
     (E) ⅕

Review your answers to practice test 1

1 **Answer (C) is correct: 1:9**
   Step 1: Put the two percentages as a ratio:
   4:36

   Step 2: Calculate the highest common denominator:
   highest common denominator = largest number that both 4
   and 36 are divisible by

   Step 3: Divide by the highest common denominator:
   4/4 : 36/4 = 1:9

2 **Answer (A) is correct:** $9/20$
   Step 1: Change the percentages to a fraction:
   18%:40% = 18/40

   Step 2: Calculate the highest common denominator:
   highest common denominator = 2
   $18/2 = 9$
   $40/2 = 20$
   fraction = $9/20$

3 **Answer (E) is correct:**
   Calculate the percentage figure:
   55 GWh $\times$ 2%/100% = 1.1 GWh

4 **Answer (A) is correct: 1:1**
   Do not be distracted by the production figure provided. The
   calculation does not require you to use this figure.

   Step 1: Calculate the total percentage for gas and renewable
   sources:
   36% + 4% = 40%

   Step 2: Calculate the ratio:
   40% : 40% = 1:1

5 **Answer (C) is correct:** $2/5$
   Convert percentage into a fraction:
   40% = $2/5$
   There is no need to calculate the figure in GWh for electricity generated by coal.

Numerical critical reasoning practice test 2

	Year 1 Sales (£100,000s)	Year 2 Sales (£100,000s)	Year 3 Sales (£100,000s)
Region a	1.82	1.64	1.29
Region b	0.45	0.52	0.31
Region c	5.37	6.11	5.91
Region d	5.20	5.86	5.88
Region e	2.34	2.79	2.05

1 In which three regions did sales decrease between Year 1 and Year 3?
   (A) a,b,c
   (B) a,b,d
   (C) a,b,e
   (D) b,c,d
   (E) b,c,e

2 In which region was there the greatest proportionate change in sales value between Year 2 and Year 3?
   (A) Region a
   (B) Region b
   (C) Region c
   (D) Region d
   (E) Region e

3 Which region had the highest sales in Years 1, 2 and 3?
   (A) Region a
   (B) Region b
   (C) Region c
   (D) Region d
   (E) Region e

4 What was the average regional sales across Regions a to d in Year 2 (in £100,000s)?
   (A) 3.50
   (B) 3.51

(C) 3.52

(D) 3.53

(E) 3.54

5   In Year 1 there were 41 sales personnel in Region e. What was the average sale per employee?

(A) £6,000

(B) £7,500

(C) £10,000

(D) £15,000

(E) £50,000

Review your answers to practice test 2

1   **Answer (C) is correct: a,b,e**
A quick review of the table will reveal those three regions where sales decreased between Year 1 and Year 3.

2   **Answer (B) is correct: Region b**
Calculate the percentage change in sales value for each region between Year 1 and Year 3:
Note that the question specifies Year 2 – Year 1 (the first column shown in the table):

Region a = $(1.29 - 1.64)/1.64 = 21.3\%$ decrease
Region b = $(0.31 - 0.52)/0.52 = 40.4\%$ decrease
Region c = $(5.91 - 6.11)/6.11 = 3.3\%$ decrease
Region d = $(5.88 - 5.86)/5.88 = 0.34\%$ increase
Region e = $(2.05 - 2.79)/2.79 = 26.5\%$ decrease

3   **Answer (C) is correct: Region c**
A quick review of the table will reveal which region was the highest regional performer in Year 1, Year 2 and Year 3.

4   **Answer (D) is correct: 3.53**
Step 1: Total the sales for Regions A to D:
Some care is needed here with ensuring that Year 2 figures are used, and that the average of 4 – not 5 – regions is required.
$1.64 + 0.52 + 6.11 + 5.86 = 14.13$

Step 2: Calculate the average:
$14.13/4 = 3.53$

5   **Answer (A) is correct: £6,000**
$2.34/41 = 0.06$ (in £100,000s) $= £6,000$

Numerical critical reasoning practice test 3

	Current budget ($)	Cut for next year
Team A	900	5%
Team B	1350	12%
Team C	400	7.5%
Team D	750	8%
Team E	1500	12.5%

1   At an exchange rate of $1.46 to the £ what is the total budget cut for next year (to the nearest £)?
    (A) £320
    (B) £332
    (C) £342
    (D) £350
    (E) £375

2   For which team(s) will next year's budget be cut by over $200?
    (A) Teams B and C
    (B) Teams B and E
    (C) Team B
    (D) Team C
    (E) None of these

3   What is the overall percentage cut in next year's budget (for all five teams)?
    (A) 9.9%
    (B) 9.6%
    (C) 4.7%
    (D) 1.9%
    (E) 0.8%

4   Next year, instead of the percentage cuts shown, a constant
    $150 deduction is made to the budgets of Teams C, D and
    E. What is next year budget's total across these three teams?
    (A) $1,600
    (B) $1,700
    (C) $1,800
    (D) $1,900
    (E) $2,200

5   What fraction is the smallest of the five team budgets of the
    largest team budget?
    (A) $\frac{2}{15}$
    (B) $\frac{1}{5}$
    (C) $\frac{4}{15}$
    (D) $\frac{1}{3}$
    (E) $\frac{6}{15}$

Review your answers to practice test 3

1   **Answer (B) is correct: £332 (to the nearest £)**
    Step 1: Calculate total budget cut for next year:
    $(900 \times 5\%) + (1{,}350 \times 12\%) + (400 \times 7.5\%) + (750 \times 8\%) + (1{,}500 \times 12.5\%)$
    $= 45 + 162 + 30 + 60 + 187.5$
    $= \$484.50$

    Step 2: Convert to £:
    exchange rate = $1.46
    $484.50/1.46 = 331.8

2   **Answer (E) is correct: None of these**
    You can use the individual calculations for Question 1.

3   **Answer (A) is correct: 9.9%**
    Using the calculations from Question 1 again:
    total cut = $484.50

    Step 1: Find the current budget total:
    $900 + $1,350 + $400 + $750 + $1,500 = $4,900

    Step 2: Find the percentage budget cut:
    $100 \times \$484.50/\$4{,}900 = 9.9\%$

4   **Answer E is correct: $2,200**
    Step 1: Add the three budgets for the current year:
    $400 + 750 + 1,500 = \$2{,}650$

    Step 2: Find the total budget deduction: $3 \times \$150 = \$450$

    Step 3: Subtract *Step 2* answer from *Step 1* answer to give next year's budget:
    $2,650 − £450 = $2,200

5   **Answer (C) is correct:** $4/15$
    $400/1{,}500 = 4/15$

Numerical critical reasoning practice test 4

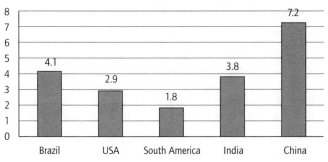

Oil demand in 2008 (million barrels per day)

1   What is the ratio of South American to Chinese oil demand?
    (A) 1:2
    (B) 1:3
    (C) 1:4
    (D) 1:5
    (E) 1:6

2   Which of the countries shown will have an oil demand in 2009
    in excess of 4.4 million barrels per day if each country experi-
    ences a 15% increase in oil demand from 2008 to 2009?
    (A) None of these
    (B) USA, China, India and Brazil
    (C) China
    (D) Brazil and China
    (E) China, India and Brazil

3   Oil demand in 2009 decreases 24% across each country. Put
    the countries in order of their decreasing oil demand.
    (A) China, Brazil, USA, India, South America
    (B) Brazil, China, India, USA, South America
    (C) China, Brazil, India, South America, USA
    (D) China, India, Brazil, USA, South America
    (E) China, Brazil, India, USA, South America

4   Which three countries combined have an oil demand of 8.8 million barrels per day in 2008?
    (A) Brazil, USA, South America
    (B) India, USA, South America
    (C) China, India, South America
    (D) China, Europe, India
    (E) China, USA, South America

5   What is the typical quarterly total number of barrels consumed by the five countries? Assume 30 days in a month and three months in a quarter.
    (A) 1,600 million
    (B) 1,700 million
    (C) 1,800 million
    (D) 1,900 million
    (E) 2,000 million

Review your answers to practice test 4

1   **Answer (C) is correct: 1:4**
    Ratio of South American to Chinese oil demand = 1.8:7.2
    = 1:4

2   **Answer (D) is correct: Brazil and China**

---

brilliant tip

This is one of those questions where you can easily eliminate answer
options. Before doing any calculations you can tell just from looking
at the graph that there are only three countries in contention:

... You know that China has to be in the answer (oil demand = 7.2)

... You then need to calculate which of Brazil and India qualify:

Brazil: $4.1 \times 115/100 = 4.715$

India: $3.8 \times 115/100 = 4.37$

---

3   **Answer (E) is correct: China, Brazil, India, USA,
    South America**
    The 24% decrease across each country is irrelevant. The
    same percentage decrease applies across all the countries.
    Hence the relative order of decreasing oil demand remains
    the same as shown in the graph.

4   **Answer (A) is correct: Brazil, USA, South America**

---

brilliant tip

You should be able to work out in your head which combinations of
three countries will add up to 8.8 million barrels per day. You can
exclude China's 7.2 million barrels per day straight away since its
contribution would make it too high to be included (once two other
countries were added in).

---

5   **Answer (C) is correct: 1,800 million**
     Step 1: Calculate the total daily number of barrels:
     $4.1 + 2.9 + 1.8 + 3.8 + 7.2 = 19.8$

     Step 2: Find the quarterly figure:
     $30 \times 3 \times 19.8 = 1,782$

     Step 3: To the nearest 100 million barrels:
     $1,782 = 1,800$

Numerical critical reasoning practice test 5

Pension fund shareholdings of Company Inc. shares (priced at £3.25)	Number of shares
Pension fund A	40,500
Pension fund B	36,750
Pension fund C	25,400
Pension fund D	22,300
Pension fund E	18,250

1   Which pension fund has shares worth £82,550?
    (A) Pension fund A
    (B) Pension fund B
    (C) Pension fund C
    (D) Pension fund D
    (E) Pension fund E

2   If Pension fund A's shareholding represents 20.25% of all Company Inc. shares, how many Company Inc. shares are there in total?
    (A) 19,000
    (B) 20,000
    (C) 25,000
    (D) 200,000
    (E) 250,000

3   What is the average value of the five pension funds (to the nearest £1,000)?
    (A) £93,000
    (B) £94,000
    (C) £95,000
    (D) £97,000
    (E) £99,000

4   What is the value of Pension funds A, B and C (to the nearest £1,000)?
    (A) £330,000

(B) £331,000
(C) £332,000
(D) £333,000
(E) £334,000

5   Company Inc. pays a dividend of 6p per share. What is the
    total dividend paid to Pension funds B to D (to the nearest
    £100)?
    (A) £5,000
    (B) £5,100
    (C) £5,200
    (D) £5,300
    (E) £5,400

Review your answers to practice test 5

1   **Answer (C) is correct: Pension fund C**
Calculate the value of each pension fund. Use the share value of £3.25 provided in the table. Work your way down the list until you get to the correct answer.
Pension fund A value = £3.25 × 40,500 = £131,625.00
Pension fund B value = £3.25 × 36,750 = £119,437.50
Pension fund C value = £3.25 × 25,400 = £82,550.00

2   **Answer (D) is correct: 200,000**
40,500 shares = 20.25%
100% = 40,500 × 100/20.25 = 200,000

3   **Answer (A) is correct: £93,000 (to the nearest £1,000)**
Carry on where we left off with Question 1, calculating the value of each pension fund:
Pension fund A value = £131,625.00
Pension fund B value = £119,437.50
Pension fund C value = £82,550.00
Pension fund D value = £72,475.00
Pension fund E value = £59,312.50
Average = total/5 = £465,400.00/5 = £93,080.00

4   **Answer (E) is correct: £334,000**
Step 1: Total the number of Company Inc. shares in Pension funds A, B and C:
40,500 + 36,750 + 25,400 = 102,650

Step 2: Calculate the value of Pension funds A, B and C:
102,650 × £3.25 = £333,612.50

Step 3: To the nearest £1,000:
£333,612.50 = £334,000

5   **Answer (B) is correct: £5,100**
Step 1: Total the number of Company Inc. shares in Pension funds B to D:

$36,750 + 25,400 + 22,300 = 84,450$

Step 2: Calculate the total dividend paid:
$6p \times 84,450 = £5,067$

Step 3: To the nearest £1,000:
$£5,067 = £5,100$

CHAPTER 9

Numerical data interpretation tests

Introduction to this format

Questions in this chapter follow the same format as those in Chapters 7 and 8 but represent a further advance in complexity, allowing you to continue your practice at a higher level. These practice tests are aimed at graduates.

brilliant example – Graduate sift

Corresponding with the very large number of graduates each year, there is a very wide range of numerical ability. To reflect this reality there are several levels of graduate numerical reasoning test. This chapter and the subsequent chapter represent typical and advanced graduate tests respectively. So in terms of graduate training schemes: from tests given on popular junior managerial schemes (eg retail and service industries) to the highly selective fast-track programmes and those rates as most desirable (eg management consulting, NHS graduate training schemes). Graduate roles in IT and banks where a higher level of numerical and/or critical thinking is necessary will also tend to use numerical reasoning tests in the later chapters of this book.

Advanced numerical data interpretation tests are often the first sift on graduate training scheme applications. You need to pass to be invited to attend the assessment centre, or to undergo a telephone interview – after which those graduate applicants who pass are invited to attend a final assessment centre.

▶

Sometimes, to check that applicants haven't cheated on such an early sift, you could be re-tested on a longer version of your first advanced numerical data interpretation test. It may be tempting to ask a maths-whizz friend to take the numerical reasoning test on your behalf. Test publishers will ask you to agree to an 'honesty contract' before your test starts online and, if you have been given SHL's Verify tests, then – as the test name suggests – your score is *verified* by checking it against your performance when taking a longer version of SHL's Verify numerical reasoning test as part of your assessment.

Guidance for numerical data interpretation tests

For ease of use, this chapter's practice questions have been grouped into sets of 5 questions. Answering all 5 questions and then reviewing your answers will help to keep you engaged during your practice sessions. Completing all the test questions should highlight to you the type of questions that you find easy and those that for the time being are more difficult. Focus your practice on the latter type of questions so as to improve your overall performance.

You are advised to:

● allow yourself 10 minutes to complete each set of 5 questions;

● read each question carefully – twice if necessary;

● choose the correct answer from the multiple-choice options shown;

● check your answers against the answer explanations that follow the test once you have completed all 5 questions;

● do this before you move on to the next test so that you can apply anything you have learnt immediately – this will aid your memory;

● use a calculator to answer the questions.

brilliant tips

● Keep things simple whenever possible so that you can focus on getting the calculation correct.

● Don't be distracted by complex business language, the size of the figures or the measurement units. Nine times out of ten the measurement units will be constant throughout the question and answer.

● Also, if you can get the right answer by doing a rough calculation then by all means do so.

● Similarly, if you can get to the answer by looking at trends in the graph then great! Rather than spending valuable time on a calculation, you may only need to scan the graph to see where, for example, the biggest and smallest differences occur.

● If you cannot decide upon an answer then try to eliminate some answer options and indicate which you think could be the correct answer.

Numerical data interpretation practice test 1

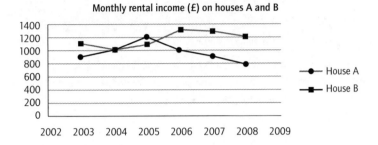

Monthly rental income (£) on houses A and B

1   What is the change in House B's monthly rental income between 2003 and 2004?
    (A) £100 increase
    (B) £100 decrease
    (C) £150 increase
    (D) £150 decrease
    (E) £200 increase

2   What is the overall change in House A's monthly rental income between 2004 and 2006?
    (A) £300 decrease
    (B) £200 decrease
    (C) £0
    (D) £200 increase
    (E) £300 increase

3   What is the difference in House B's annual rental income for 2007 compared to 2003?
    (A) £0
    (B) £1,200
    (C) £2,400
    (D) £4,800
    (E) £7,200

4   What is the difference in House B's monthly rental income for 2008 compared to 2003?

(A) £100 less (per month)

(B) £100 more (per month)

(C) £200 less (per month)

(D) £200 more (per month)

(E) No difference

5   For which two years is there a difference of £400 in rental income for House A compared to House B?

(A) 2003, 2006

(B) 2005, 2006

(C) 2006, 2007

(D) 2007, 2008

(E) 2006, 2008

Review your answers to practice test 1

1   **Answer (B) is correct: £100 decrease**
£1,100 (in 2003) − £1,000 (in 2004) = £100 increase

2   **Answer (C) is correct: £0**
£1,000 (in 2006) − £1,000 (in 2004) = £0 increase

3   **Answer (C) is correct: £2,400**
Calculate the total difference in rental income for each year:
2003: 1,100 × 12 = £13,200
2007: 1,300 × 12 = £15,600
£15,600 − £13,200 = £2,400

4   **Answer (A) is correct: £100 less (per month)**
Calculate the difference between the two graph readings:
2008 = £1,200 per month
2003 = £1,100 per month
Difference = £1,200 − £1,100 = £100 less (per month)

5   **Answer (D) is correct: 2007, 2008**

Numerical data interpretation practice test 2

	MAGAZINES A-E				
	A	B	C	D	E
Annual fee (£)	49.00	59.00	54.99	55.99	49.99
Monthly fee (£)	5.00	6.00	5.49	5.99	4.99

1   What is the cost of taking out monthly subscriptions for 18 months with Magazines A, B and D?
(A) £74.99
(B) £88.50
(C) £265.93
(D) £305.82
(E) £323.64

2   What is the total cost of six months subscription to all five magazines?
(A) £161.82
(B) £164.82
(C) £167.82
(D) £170.82
(E) £173.82

3   Which magazine offers the greatest saving in taking out an annual subscription rather than a monthly subscription?
(A) Magazine A
(B) Magazine B
(C) Magazine C
(D) Magazine D
(E) Magazine E

4   Which magazine offers the least saving in taking out an annual subscription rather than a monthly subscription?
(A) Magazine A
(B) Magazine B
(C) Magazine C

(D) Magazine D

(E) Magazine E

5   The cost of monthly contract 'a' rises by 15%. What is the
     new cost of six monthly payments?

(A) £30.00

(B) £32.50

(C) £34.50

(D) £35.00

(E) £36.50

Review your answers to practice test 2

1   **Answer (D) is correct: £305.82**
Step 1: Calculate the total monthly cost for all three magazines:
£5.00 + £6.00 + £5.99 = £16.99

Step 2: Calculate the cost for 18 months:
£16.99 × 18 = £305.82
Note that the question stresses monthly subscriptions. The answer option £265.93 is the correct answer if the calculation were six monthly subscriptions, together with an annual subscription (for the other 12 months).

⁂brilliant tips

● This question can be answered in two steps only - rather than doing three separate calculations for the three magazines. Make the addition calculation first (£5.00 + £6.00 + £5.99). Then the total cost for 18 months.

● Another short cut is to calculate 17 × 18 and then deduct the 18p from your total.

2   **Answer (B) is correct: £164.82**
6 × (£5.00 + £6.00 + £5.49 + £5.99 + £4.99) = £164.82

3   **Answer (D) is correct: Magazine D**
Step 1: Calculate each subscription's total monthly cost for a year's worth of monthly payments:
Magazine A = 12 × £5.00 = £60.00
Magazine B = 12 × £6.00 = £72.00
Magazine C = 12 × £5.49 = £65.88
Magazine D = 12 × £5.99 = £71.88
Magazine E = 12 × £4.99 = £59.88

Step 2: Calculate the difference for each subscription with the annual fee:

Magazine A = £60.00 − £49.00 = £11.00
Magazine B = £72.00 − £59.00 = £13.00
Magazine C = £65.88 − £54.99 = £10.89
Magazine D = £71.88 − £55.99 = £15.89
Magazine E = £59.88 − £49.99 = £9.89

4   **Answer (E) is correct: Magazine E**

5   **Answer (C) is correct: £34.50**
Step 1: Calculate the new monthly fee:
£5.00 × 115%/100% = £5.75

Step 2: Calculate the cost for six months:
£5.75 × 6 = £34.50

Numerical data interpretation practice test 3

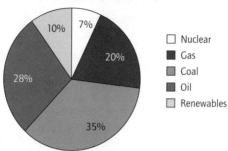

2008 Australian electricity demand
(million tonnes of oil equivalent)

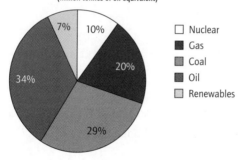

2050 Australian electricity demand
(million tonnes of oil equivalent)

1   What is the 2008 demand ratio between gas, renewables and coal?
   (A) 2:1:3
   (B) 3:2:5
   (C) 3:2:7
   (D) 4:2:5
   (E) 4:2:7

2   What fraction of total electricity production for 2008 are gas and coal, respectively?
   (A) $\frac{1}{5}$; $\frac{7}{20}$
   (B) $\frac{7}{20}$; $\frac{1}{5}$
   (C) $\frac{1}{3}$; $\frac{7}{20}$

(D) $^7/_{10}$; $^1/_2$

(E) $^1/_3$; $^7/_{10}$

3   The total Australian electricity demand is 280 billion kWh in 2008. How much of this is produced by gas

(A) 28 billion kWh

(B) 42 billion kWh

(C) 56 billion kWh

(D) 70 billion kWh

(E) 84 billion kWh

4   Between 2008 and 2050 the size of Australian electricity demand from renewable is forecast to change by what percentage?

(A) 3% more

(B) 3% less

(C) 13% more

(D) 13% less

(E) 10% less

5   Between 2008 and 2050 which form of electricity generation exhibits the least change?

(A) Gas

(B) Nuclear

(C) Coal

(D) Oil

(E) Renewables

Review your answers to practice test 3

1 **Answer (E) is correct: 4:2:7**
   Step 1: Put percentage as a ratio:
   20:10:35

   Step 2: Simplify the ratio:
   4:2:7

2 **Answer (A) is correct: $\frac{1}{5}$; $\frac{7}{20}$**
   Step 1: Convert each percentage to a fraction:
   Gas 20% = 20/100
   Coal 35% = 35/100

   Step 2: Simplify fractions by dividing by highest common
   denominator:
   gas (highest common denominator = 20)
   $20/120 = (20/20)/(120/20) = \frac{1}{5}$
   coal (highest common denominator = 5)
   $35/100 = (35/5)/(100/5) = \frac{7}{20}$

3 **Answer (C) is correct: 56 billion kWh**
   Step 1: Read percentage from 2008 pie chart:
   gas = 20%

   Step 2: Calculate percentage amount using the total production figure supplied:
   $280 \times 20/100 = 56$ billion kWh

4 **Answer (B) is correct: 3% less**
   The change from 10% to 7% represents 3% less.

5 **Answer (A) is correct: Gas**

Numerical data interpretation practice test 4

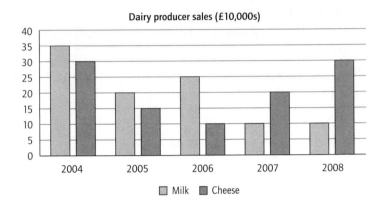

Dairy producer sales (£10,000s)

1   The projected milk sales for 2009 are 1.08 times higher than those for 2008. What would this make the total milk sales between 2005 and 2009 (in £10,000s)?
   (A) 75.8
   (B) 88.00
   (C) 90.8
   (D) 95.8
   (E) 105.00

2   In which two years was there the same combined production of cheese and milk?
   (A) 2004 and 2006
   (B) 2005 and 2006
   (C) 2006 and 2007
   (D) 2007 and 2008
   (E) 2008 and 2004

3   What were the average annual cheese sales across the five years shown?
   (A) 200,000
   (B) 205,000
   (C) 210,000

(D) 215,000

(E) 220,000

4   In which year was there the greatest difference between cheese and milk sales?

(A) 2004

(B) 2005

(C) 2006

(D) 2007

(E) 2008

5   In which year was the combined value of milk and cheese sales equal to £400,000?

(A) 2004

(B) 2005

(C) 2006

(D) 2007

(E) 2008

Review your answers to practice test 4

1   **Answer (A) is correct: 75.8**
Step 1: Calculate the total milk sales for 2005 (note not 2004) to 2008:

> ☀️**brilliant** tip
>
> Ignore the £10,000s since this will be constant throughout your calculation.

20 + 25 + 10 + 10 = 65

Step 2: Calculate the sales for 2009:
$10 \times 108/100 = 10.8$

Step 3:
Total milk sales 2005–2009 = 65 + 10.8 = 75.8

2   **Answer (B) is correct: 2005 and 2006**
You can exclude 2004 just from looking at the graph – both milk and cheese sales are higher than for any other year:
2005 cheese and milk sales = 20 + 15 = 35
2006 cheese and milk sales = 25 + 10 = 35
2007 cheese and milk sales = 10 + 20 = 30
2008 cheese and milk sales = 10 + 30 = 40

3   **Answer (C) is correct: 210,000**
Step 1:
Find the total cheese sales across the five years shown:
30 + 15 + 10 + 20 + 30 = 1,050,000

Step 2: Find the average:
1,050,000/5 = 210,000

4   **Answer (E) is correct: 2008**
You need to look for the largest 'gap' between the cheese and milk sales on the graph.

5   **Answer (E) is correct: 2008**
      You need to review the milk and cheese values on the graph,
      adding the two figures together for each year (ideally to save
      time in your head).

Numerical data interpretation practice test 5

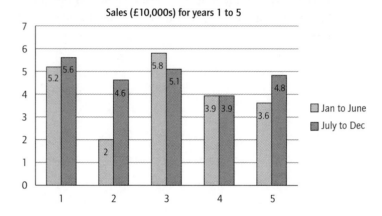

Sales (£10,000s) for years 1 to 5

1   What is the difference in the total sales for Years 1–2 and
     Years 3–5 (in £10,000s)?
     (A) 8.7
     (B) 9.7
     (C) 10.7
     (D) 87
     (E) 97

2   In an audit the Year 3 sales are discovered to be 4% too high.
     What is the correct figure (to the nearest £1,000)?
     (A) £94,000
     (B) £104,000
     (C) £105,000
     (D) £114,000
     (E) £115,000

3   In which year was the half-yearly sales greater between
     January and June than between July and December?
     (A) Year 1
     (B) Year 2
     (C) Year 3

(D) Year 4

(E) Year 5

4   In which year was there an increase in January–June sales compared to the previous year?

(A) Year 1

(B) Year 2

(C) Year 3

(D) Year 4

(E) Year 5

5   What were the average monthly sales in Years 1–4 between January and June?

(A) £40,000

(B) £40,215

(C) £42,225

(D) £42,250

(E) £45,520

Review your answers to practice test 5

1   **Answer (B) is correct: 9.7**
    Step 1: Find the total sales for Years 1–2 and for Years 3–5:
    Years 1–2: 5.2 + 2 + 5.6 + 4.6 = 17.4
    Years 3–5: 5.8 + 5.1 + 3.9 + 3.9 + 3.6 + 4.8 = 27.1

    Step 2: Find the difference:
    27.1 − 17.4 = 9.7

2   **Answer (C) is correct: £105,000**
    Year 3 sales − 4% = (5.8 + 5.1) × 96/100 = £104,640

3   **Answer (C) is correct: Year 3**
    Look at the graph to see where the January–June figures are
    above the July–December figures.

4   **Answer (C) is correct: Year 3**
    Look at the graph to see where there has been an increase
    in January–June sales.

5   **Answer (D) is correct: £42,250**
    Step 1: Total the January–June sales (Years 1–4):
    5.2 + 2 + 5.8 + 3.9 = 16.9

    Step 2: Find the average:
    16.9/4 = 4.225

    Step 3: Convert from (£10,000s):
    4.225 × £10,000 = £42,250

Numerical data interpretation practice test 6

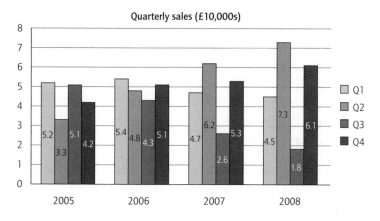

Quarterly sales (£10,000s)

1   If the total cost of sales in 2008 was £87,000 what was the
    profit (where profit = total sales – total cost of sales)
    (A) £197,000
    (B) £190,000
    (C) £117,000
    (D) £110,000
    (E) £107,000

2   What was the overall percentage increase in Quarter 4 sales
    between years 2005 and 2008 (to the nearest %)?
    (A) 45%
    (B) 50%
    (C) 54%
    (D) 55%
    (E) 65%

3   In which year and which quarter was there the lowest quar-
    terly sales?
    (A) Q2 2005
    (B) Q3 2007
    (C) Q1 2008

(D) Q3 2008
(E) Q2 2008

4   Between which two quarters was there the largest change in sales?
(A) Q3–Q4 2006
(B) Q3–Q4 2007
(C) Q3–Q4 2008
(D) Q2–Q3 2008
(E) Q2–Q3 2006

5   What were Quarter 1 and Quarter 3's sales in the two-year period 2006–2007 combined?
(A) £150,000
(B) £160,000
(C) £170,000
(D) £180,000
(E) £200,000

Review your answers to practice test 6

1   **Answer (D) is correct: £110,000**
    Step 1: Find the total sales:
    £45,000 + £73,000 + £18,000 + £61,000 = £197,000

    Step 2: Profit = total sales − total cost of sales:
    £197,000 − £87,000 = £110,000

2   **Answer (A) is correct: 45%**
    100% × (6.1 − 4.2)/4.2 = 45.2%

3   **Answer (D) is correct: Q3 2008**
    Review the graph to see where there is the lowest value then read off the year and the quarter.

4   **Answer (D) is correct: Q2–Q3 2008**
    Review the graph to see where there have been large increases or decreases in sales.
    Work out the value of those that could be the largest shown, e.g.
    Q2–Q3 2007 = 6.2 − 2.6 = 3.6
    Q3–Q4 2007 = 5.3 − 2.6 = 2.7
    Q2–Q3 2008 = 7.3 − 1.8 = 5.5
    Q3–Q4 2008 = 6.1 − 1.8 = 4.3

5   **Answer (C) is correct: £170,000**
    Step 1: Total Q1 sales:
    5.4 + 4.7 = 10.1

    Step 2: Total Q2 sales:
    4.3 + 2.6 = 6.9

    Step 3: Add Q1 and Q2 sales totals:
    10.1 + 6.9 = 17 (£10,000s) = £170,000

Numerical data interpretation practice test 7

Clothes shop sales (£10,000s)

☐ Brand A   ▨ Brand B   ■ Brand C

1   Which months have seen consecutive increases in both Brand A and Brand B sales?
    (A) Jan, Feb
    (B) Feb, March
    (C) March, April
    (D) April, May
    (E) None of these

2   In which months were the total sales in excess of £171,000?
    (A) April
    (B) March
    (C) May
    (D) March and April
    (E) None of these

3   In which month was the ratio of sales from Brands A:B:C in the ratio 4:3:1?
    (A) January
    (B) February
    (C) March
    (D) April
    (E) May

4   What is the difference between February's Brand A and Brand C sales?

(A) £3,500
(B) £4,000
(C) £4,500
(D) £5,000
(E) £5,500

5   What was the average monthly Brand B sales figure between
     January and April? (to the nearest £1,000)
     (A) £51,000
     (B) £52,000
     (C) £53,000
     (D) £54,000
     (E) £55,000

Review your answers to practice test 7

1   **Answer (C) is correct: March, April**

Review the graph to see where there has been a consecutive increase in sales for Brand A. Then see if for those months there has also been a consecutive increase in sales for Brand B sales.

2   **Answer (E) is correct: None of these**

Calculate the total sales for each month:
January: 6.2 + 2 + 4 = 12.2
February: 5.6 + 4.6 + 5.1 = 15.3
March: 7.1 + 6.2 + 3.6 = 16.9
April: 10 + 7.75 + 2.25 = 20
May: 8 + 4.3 + 4.3 = 16.6

3   **Answer (D) is correct: April**

Review the graphs for a 4:3:1 pattern, i.e. Brand A is four times the size of Brand C and Brand B is three times the size of Brand C.

4   **Answer (D) is correct: £5,000**

Step 1: Find the difference in February's Brand A and Brand C sales:
5.6 − 5.1 = 0.5

Step 2: Convert to £10,000s:
0.5 × £10,000 = £5,000

5   **Answer (A) is correct: £51,000**

Step 1: Sum the Brand B sales for the four months January–April
2 + 4.6 + 6.2 + 7.5 = 20.3

Step 2: Average this sum:
20.3/4 = 5.075

Step 3: To the nearest £1,000:
£51,000

CHAPTER 10

Advanced
numerical
data
interpretation

Introduction to this format

Tests of advanced numerical data interpretation are one of the most difficult forms of numerical reasoning test. Although these questions share a similar format with the graduate-level questions in the previous chapters, this range is benchmarked at a higher level. These questions are more difficult since at least two or more calculations – or more – are needed typically per question. These are not necessarily complex calculations.

The questions are designed to mirror the type of numerical problems that managers face in the workplace and are set within an organisational context. So you are being assessed on applying your numeracy skills to business data. Many of the practice questions are set within the context of a (fictitious) international company called Conglomerate plc. From the table(s)/graph(s) presented you must 'find' the data you need to answer the question.

Guidance for advanced data interpretation practice tests

The practice questions appear in sets of 4–6. Each of these is followed by its respective answer explanations.

Start off by deciding what data you need and which of the graphs and/or tables contains it. Then locate the specific data that you need.

You are advised to:

● aim for roughly 1–2 minutes per question since questions can have 1, 2, 3 or more calculation stages;

● check your answers against the answer explanations that follow the test once you have completed all the questions;

● do this before you move on to the next test so that you can apply anything you have learnt immediately – this will aid your memory;

● use a calculator to answer the questions.

✷ brilliant tips

● For this question type the number of calculations in a question is high, which greatly increases the opportunity for error.

● Keep things simple whenever possible so that you can focus on getting the calculation correct.

● Don't go for an answer just because it is the closest to your own calculation. The question will specify if you need to round up an answer.

● Don't be distracted by complex business language, the size of the figures or the measurement units. Nine times out of ten the measurement units will be constant throughout the question and answer.

● If you can get the right answer by doing a rough calculation then by all means do so.

● You can in some cases simplify things for yourself – for example, focus on the one-to-nine digits in each figure rather on the zeroes (tens, hundreds, thousands, millions even) that follow the digits.

● You can also simplify matters by working to one decimal point, thus cutting down on the number of digits you need to write down and manipulate.

Advanced data interpretation practice test 1

Conglomerate plc turnover by world region	2006 (£ millions)	2007 (£ millions)	2008 (£ millions)
Asia-Pacific	280.8	282.3	292.2
UK	479.3	482.5	477.9
North America	341	352.7	364.5
South America	180.3	133.9	86.7
Rest of world	139.2	162.2	174.7
Total	1,420.6	1,413.6	1,396.0

Conglomerate plc worldwide turnover by market sector	2006 (£ millions)	2007 (£ millions)	2008 (£ millions)
Retail	314.5	318.2	321.9
Leisure markets	173.1	164.6	161.8
Packaging	469.2	474.9	467.6
Food markets	411.6	403.1	392.3
Other markets	52.2	52.8	52.4
Total	1,420.6	1,413.6	1,396.0

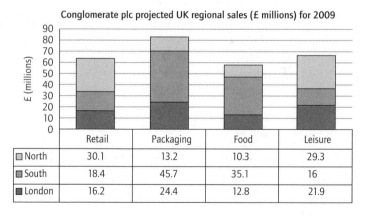

Conglomerate plc projected UK regional sales (£ millions) for 2009

	Retail	Packaging	Food	Leisure
North	30.1	13.2	10.3	29.3
South	18.4	45.7	35.1	16
London	16.2	24.4	12.8	21.9

1   How many world regions and market sectors have shown an annual turnover increase for the years 2007 and 2008?

(A) 1 world region; 1 market sector

(B) 1 world region; 2 market sectors

(C) 2 world regions; 1 market sector

(D) 2 world regions; 2 market sectors

(E) 3 world regions; 1 market sector

2 Which market sector and which world region have shown
   the lowest absolute change between 2006 and 2008?
   (A) South America, Retail
   (B) Asia-Pacific, Packaging
   (C) Other markets, Packaging
   (D) UK, Other markets
   (E) UK, Packaging

3 What approximate percentage change in UK regional sales
   is predicted from 2008 to 2009?
   (A) None of these
   (B) 43% decrease
   (C) 43% increase
   (D) 75% decrease
   (E) 75% increase

4 What is the absolute difference (in £ millions) between the
   highest and the lowest performing market sectors (highest
   and lowest turnovers) between 2006 and 2008?
   (A) £7.4 million
   (B) £19.3 million
   (C) £26.7 million
   (D) £29.3 million
   (E) £30.7 million

5 What are the total projected sales for 2009 in the Northern
   and Southern regions?
   (A) £140.5 million
   (B) £158.2 million
   (C) £190.5 million
   (D) £198.1 million
   (E) £273.4 million

Review your answers to practice test 1

1   **Answer (E) is correct: 3 world regions; 1 market sector**
    Where's the information I need? Look in: *Conglomerate plc turnover by world region* and *Conglomerate plc worldwide turnover by market sector* tables.
    Count up the number of regions and sectors that have increased between 2006 and 2007, 2007 and 2008:
    Asia-Pacific, North America, Rest of World = 3 world regions
    Retail = 1 market sector

2   **Answer (D) is correct: UK, Other markets**
    Where's the information I need? Look in: *Conglomerate plc turnover by world region* and *Conglomerate plc worldwide turnover by market sector* tables.
    Calculate the difference between the 2006 and 2008 figures for each world region and each market sector:

brilliant tip

Absolute change means that you can ignore where the change has been an increase or a decrease.

Asia-Pacific = 292.2 − 280.8 = 11.4
UK = 477.9 − 479.3= −1.4
North America = 364.5 − 341 = 23.5
South America = 180.3 − 86.7 = 93.6
Rest of world = 174.7 − 139.2 = 35.5
Retail = 321.9 − 314.5 = 7.4
Leisure markets = 161.8 − 173.1 = − 11.3
Packaging = 467.6 − 469.2 = −1.6
Food markets = 392.3 − 411.6 = −19.3
Other markets = 52.4 − 52.2 = 0.2

3   **Answer (B) is correct: 43% decrease**
Where's the information I need? Look in: *Conglomerate plc turnover by world region* table and *Conglomerate plc projected UK regional sales (£ millions) for 2009* graph.

Step 1: The 2008 figure for the UK, £477.9 million, can be read directly from the *Conglomerate plc turnover by world region* table.

Step 2: Find the sum of the projected UK regional sales figures:
London total + Southern total + Northern total
75.3 + 115.2 + 82.9 = 273.4

Step 3: Find the difference:
477.9 − 273.4 = 204.5

Step 4: Turn this into a percentage:
100% × 204.5/477.9 = 43% (rounded up)

4   **Answer (C) is correct: £26.7 million**
Where's the information I need? Look in: *Conglomerate plc worldwide turnover by market sector* table.

Step 1: You need to calculate the difference in sales for each market sector between 2006 and 2008. This has already been done for Question 2. The most profitable sector is Retail (£7.4 million increase in sales). The least profitable sector is Food markets (£19.3 million drop in sales).

Step 2: Difference = 19.3 + 7.4 = £26.7 million

5   **Answer (D) is correct: £198.1 million**
Where's the information I need? Look in: *Conglomerate plc Projected UK regional sales (£ millions)* table.
Add the projected sales for the Northern and the Southern regions: £82.9 + £115.2 = £198.1 million

Advanced data interpretation practice test 2

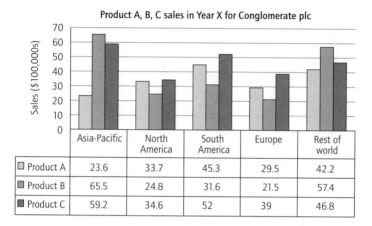

Product A, B, C sales in Year X for Conglomerate plc

	Asia-Pacific	North America	South America	Europe	Rest of world
Product A	23.6	33.7	45.3	29.5	42.2
Product B	65.5	24.8	31.6	21.5	57.4
Product C	59.2	34.6	52	39	46.8

Conglomerate plc world regions operational source	New customer packaging sales for 2008 ($100,000s)
Asia-Pacific	7.2
Europe	5.3
North America	4.2
South America	8.1
Rest of world	3.5

Conglomerate plc total packaging sales ($100,000s) for 2008 (including new customer packaging sales)

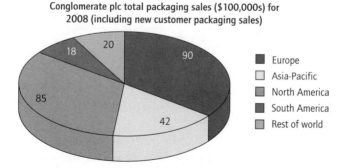

Conglomerate plc operational source

1   The worldwide target for Product A sales is $18 million.
    From sales levels in Year x, by how much approximately do
    Product A sales need to increase to reach this target?
    (A) $20,000
    (B) $200,000
    (C) $0.4 million
    (D) $0.6 million
    (E) $0.8 million

2   Which two regions together have combined Product A, B
    and C sales in Year x that are less than $22 million?
    (A) Rest of world, North America
    (B) Europe, South America
    (C) Europe, North America
    (D) North America, South America
    (E) Europe, Rest of world

3   What are the total new customer packaging sales for 2008?
    (A) $2.38 million
    (B) $2.63 million
    (C) $2.83 million
    (D) $2.88 million
    (E) $3.83 million

4   Which region's individual packaging sales has the highest
    percentage of new customer sales in 2008?
    (A) Asia-Pacific
    (B) Europe
    (C) North America
    (D) South America
    (E) Rest of world

5   What is the ratio of European to Rest of world total pack-
    aging sales in 2008?
    (A) 2:9
    (B) 9:2
    (C) 1:9
    (D) 9:1
    (E) 4:1

Review your answers to practice test 2

1   **Answer (D) is correct: $0.6 million**
    Where's the information I need? Look in: *Product A, B, C
    sales in Year* x graph.
    Step 1: Find the sales in Year x for Product A ($100,000s):
    23.6 + 33.7 + 45.3 + 29.5 + 42.2 = 174.3
    174.3 (in $100,000s) = $17.4 million

    Step 2: Find the difference:
    $18 million − $17.4 million = $0.6 million

2   **Answer (C) is correct: Europe, North America**
    Where's the information I need? Look in: *Product A, B, C
    sales in Year* x graph.
    Step 1: Calculate (in $100,000s to keep things simple) the
    total Product A, B and C sales for each world region shown:
    Asia-Pacific = 23.6 + 65.5 + 59.2 = 148.3
    North America = 33.7 + 24.8 + 34.6 = 93.1
    South America = 45.3 + 31.6 + 52 = 128.9
    Europe = 29.5 + 21.5 + 39 = 90
    Rest of world = 42.2 + 57.4 + 46.8 = 146.4

    Step 2: The two regions with the lowest sales (Europe, North
    America) are those that when combined have sales less than
    $22 million ($9,000,000 + $9,300,000 = $18,300,000).

3   **Answer C) is correct: $2.83 million**
    Where's the information I need? Look in: *Conglomerate plc
    world regions operational source* table.
    7.2 + 5.3 + 4.2 + 8.1 + 3.5 = $2.83 million

4   **Answer (D) is correct: South America**
    Where's the information I need? Look in: *Conglomerate plc
    world regions operational source* table and *Total packaging sales*
    pie chart.
    Calculate the percentage of new business per region:
    Asia-Pacific = 100% × 7.2/42 = 17.1%

North America = $100\% \times 4.2/85 = 4.9\%$
South America = $100\% \times 8.1/18 = 45\%$
Europe = $100\% \times 5.3/90 = 5.9\%$
Rest of world = $100\% \times 3.5/20 = 17.5\%$

5   **Answer (B) is correct: 9:2**
Where's the information I need? Look in: *Total packaging sales* pie chart.
$90:20 = 9:2$

Advanced data interpretation practice test 3

Retail sales for Product A (£10,000s)

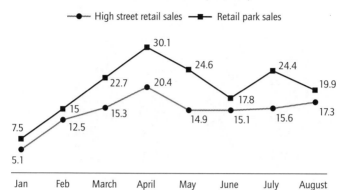

Telecommunications company
UK sales 2008 by market (£ millions)

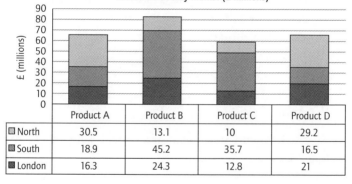

	Product A	Product B	Product C	Product D
North	30.5	13.1	10	29.2
South	18.9	45.2	35.7	16.5
London	16.3	24.3	12.8	21

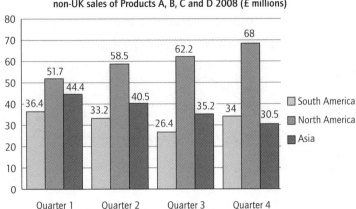

Telecommunications company
non-UK sales of Products A, B, C and D 2008 (£ millions)

1   In which two months is there the same difference between
    the high street and retail sales for Product A?
    (A) January, February
    (B) January, August
    (C) February, August
    (D) None of these
    (E) April, May

2   In which month were high street retail sales higher than
    retail park sales for Product A?
    (A) None of these
    (B) January
    (C) February
    (D) July
    (E) August

3   Between which months did both the retail park and high
    street sales of Product A fall?
    (A) February to March
    (B) March to April
    (C) April to May

(D) May to June

(E) June to July

4   In 2008 what is the difference between the UK and Asian sales (to the nearest £ million)?

(A) £113 million

(B) £123 million

(C) £133 million

(D) £143 million

(E) £153 million

5   In which two quarters were the total non-UK sales the same?

(A) Quarter 1, Quarter 2

(B) Quarter 1, Quarter 3

(C) Quarter 1, Quarter 4

(D) Quarter 2, Quarter 3

(E) Quarter 3, Quarter 4

6   Due to increasing inflation, 2009's quarterly non-UK sales are predicted to be 3%, 4%, 5% and 6% higher than the respective 2008 quarters. What is the total sales prediction for 2009?

(A) £544.4 million

(B) £555.5 million

(C) £566.6 million

(D) £577.7 million

(E) £588.8 million

Review your answers to practice test 3

1   **Answer (E) is correct: April, May**
    Where's the information I need? Look in: *Retail sales for Product A (£10,000s) graph.*
    Work out the differences, as follows:

Jan	5.1	7.5	2.4
Feb	12.5	15	2.5
March	15.3	22.7	7.4
April	20.4	30.1	9.7
May	14.9	24.6	9.7
June	15.1	17.8	2.7
July	15.6	24.4	8.8
August	17.3	19.9	2.6

2   **Answer (A) is correct: None of these**
    Where's the information I need? Look in: *Retail sales for Product A (£10,000s) graph.*
    The line graph for Retail park sales is above the line graph for high street retail sales for each month shown.

3   **Answer (C) is correct: April to May**
    Where's the information I need? Look in: *Retail sales for Product A (£10,000s) graph.*
    Review this to establish when the line graph for Retail park sales and the line graph for high street retail sales are both sloping downwards.

4   **Answer (B) is correct: £123 million**
    Where's the information I need? Look in: *Telecommunications company – non-UK sales* graph and *Telecommunications company – UK sales 2008 by market (£ millions)* graph.

    Step 1: Find the totals for UK sales and Asian sales:
    UK sales: 82.8 (North) + 116.3 (South) + 74.4 (London) = £273.5 million
    Asian sales: 44.4 + 40.5 + 35.2 + 30.5 = £150.6 million

Step 2: Find the difference (to the nearest £ million):
£273 million − £150 million = £123 million

5   **Answer (C) is correct: Quarter 1, Quarter 4**
Where's the information I need? Look in: *Telecommunications company – non-UK sales* graph.
Calculate the quarterly totals:
Quarter 1 = 132.5
Quarter 2 = 132.2
Quarter 3 = 123.8
Quarter 4 = 132.5

6   **Answer (A) is correct: £544.4 million**
Where's the information I need? Look in: *Telecommunications company – non-UK sales* graph.

Step 1: Add the relevant percentage increase to the relevant quarters:
Quarter 1: $132.5 \times 103\% = 136.48$
Quarter 2: $132.2 \times 104\% = 137.49$
Quarter 3: $123.8 \times 105\% = 129.99$
Quarter 4: $132.5 \times 106\% = 140.45$

Step 2: Add up these totals = £544.4 million

Advanced data interpretation practice test 4

Conglomerate plc UK function

	Yearly budget (£100,000s)	Quarter 1 Actual cost (£100,000s)	Quarter 2 Actual cost (£100,000s)	Quarter 3 Actual cost (£100,000s)	Quarter 4 Actual cost (£100,000s)
Sales/marketing	12	2.3	2.6	2.9	2.8
Production	35	8.8	9.5	10.1	9.1
Operations	64	15.2	15.5	16.5	17.8
Overheads	7	1.7	1.6	1.9	1.4
Rent/office expenses	24	5.9	5.8	6.4	5.7

Conglomerate plc worldwide turnover

	2006 (£ millions)	2007 (£ millions)	2008 (£ millions)
Retail	358.9	342.1	321.9
Packaging	162.3	164.1	161.8
Food	441.4	466.0	467.6
Leisure	358.2	377.6	392.3
Other markets	59.4	62.7	52.4
Total turnover	1,380.2	1,412.5	1,396

1   What is the difference between the total costs for the four quarters and the yearly budget?

(A) £1.5 million

(B) £1 million

(C) £750,000

(D) £250,000

(E) £150,000

2   Which area's quarterly costs have the highest discrepancy with the yearly budget?

(A) Sales/marketing

(B) Production

(C) Operations

(D) Overheads

(E) Rent/office expenses

3   Which of the following statements is true?

(A) Quarter 1 contributed the most to the budget overspend

(B) Production has the highest yearly budget

(C) Operational costs have been increasing between Quarter 1 and Quarter 4

(D) Worldwide turnover was highest in 2008

(E) Worldwide turnover for all three years combined was less than £4,100 million

4   Which of the following contributed the highest percentage to worldwide turnover between 2006 and 2008?

(A) Retail

(B) Packaging

(C) Food

(D) Leisure

(E) Other markets

Review your answers to practice test 4

Answer (E) is correct: £150,000

1   Where's the information I need? Look in: *Conglomerate plc UK functions* table.

Step 1:
Calculate the total costs for the four quarters:
Quarter 1 = 33.9
Quarter 2 = 35
Quarter 3 = 37.8
Quarter 4 = 36.8
Total = 143.5

Step 2: Compare with the yearly budget to find the difference: 142
143.5 − 142 = 1.5 (in £100,000's) = £150,000

2   **Answer (B) is correct: Production**
Where's the information I need? Look in: *Conglomerate plc UK functions* table.
Calculate the differences between budget and cost for each function:
Sales/marketing: 12 (budget) − 10.6 = 1.4
Production: 35 (budget) − 37.5 = −2.5
Operational: 64 (budget) − 65 = −1
Overheads: 7 (budget) − 6.6 = 0.4
Rent/office expenses: 24 (budget) − 23.8 = 0.2

3   **Answer (C) is correct: Operational costs have been increasing between Quarter 1 and Quarter 4**
Where's the information I need? Look in: *Conglomerate plc worldwide turnover (to year end)* table and *Conglomerate plc UK function* table.
Taking the statements one at a time:

(A) Quarter 1 contributed the most to the budget overspend.
    FALSE – Calculate the totals for each quarter:

Quarter 1 = 33.9
Quarter 2 = 35
Quarter 3 = 37.8
Quarter 4 = 36.8
It is Quarter 3 where the most has been spent.

(B) Production has the highest yearly budget.
FALSE – Operations has the highest yearly budget.

(C) Operational costs have been increasing between Quarter 1 and Quarter 4.
TRUE – You can see this visually from scanning the chart of figures. If you did this before going through some of the other statements (particularly statement (A)) then well done you!

(D) Worldwide turnover was highest in 2008.
FALSE – Worldwide turnover was highest in 2007.

(E) Worldwide turnover was less than £4,100 million.
FALSE – Worldwide turnover = £1,380.2 + £1,412.5 + £1,396 = £4,188.7 million

4   **Answer (C) is correct: Food**
Where's the information I need? Look in: *Conglomerate plc worldwide turnover (to year end)* table.
Think through what the question is really asking. You can reinterpret the question as 'which had the highest sales worldwide?' Hence you just need to total the sales for each:
Retail's total sales 2006–2008 = 1,022.9
Packaging's total sales 2006–2008 = 488.2
Food's total sales 2006–2008 = 1,375
Leisure's total sales 2006–2008 = 1,128.1
Other market's total sales 2006–2008 = 174.5

Advanced data interpretation practice test 5

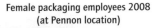

Female packaging employees 2008
(at Pennon location)

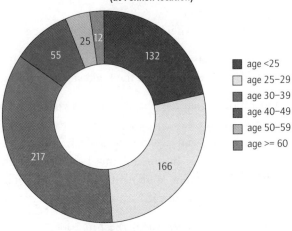

- age <25
- age 25–29
- age 30–39
- age 40–49
- age 50–59
- age >= 60

Male packaging employees 2008
(at Pennon location)

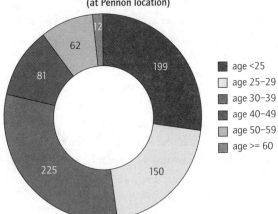

- age <25
- age 25–29
- age 30–39
- age 40–49
- age 50–59
- age >= 60

Conglomerate plc employees by function 2006–2008

	2006	2007	2008
Retail	3,580	3,973	3,855
Logistics	1,425	1,511	1,636
Packaging	1,672	1,487	1,622
Food	1,561	1,509	1,588
Leisure	2,451	2,486	2,121
Total	10,689	10,966	10,822

1 Which age band for packaging employees at Pennon con-
   tains the highest ratio of male to female employees?
   (A) <25 years
   (B) 25–29 years
   (C) 30–39 years
   (D) 40–49 years
   (E) 50–59 years

2 What is the total number of employees under 30 years of age
   at the Pennon location?
   (A) 367
   (B) 467
   (C) 647
   (D) 677
   (E) 766

3 In 2008 there are two packaging sites: at Pennon and Asle.
   How many employees work at the Asle site?
   (A) 276
   (B) 286
   (C) 296
   (D) 306
   (E) 315

4 Which function has experienced the second largest change
   in staff numbers between 2006 and 2008?
   (A) Retail

(B) Logistics

(C) Packaging

(D) Food

(E) Leisure

5   If the Retail profits in 2007 are £79.46 million what are the profits per Retail employee?

(A) £22,000

(B) £20,000

(C) £19,200

(D) £2,200

(E) £2,000

Review your answers to practice test 5

1   **Answer (E) is correct: 50–59 years**
     Where's the information I need? Look in: *Female packaging employees in 2008 (at Pennon location)* pie chart and *Male packaging employees in 2008 (at Pennon location)* pie chart. Calculate the ratio of male to female employees for each age band.

> ⚡ **brilliant tip**
>
> The ratio of male to female employees for those aged 50-59 years is far higher than for any of the other age bands. You could perhaps have got to this answer by writing down the respective numbers of male and female employees and then comparing them visually.

	Age <25	Age 25-29	Age 30-39	Age 40-49	Age 50-59
Female	132	166	217	55	25
Male	199	150	225	81	62
Ratio	199/132 = 1.51	150/166 = 0.90	225/217 = 1.04	81/55 = 1.47	62/25 = 2.48

2   **Answer (C) is correct: 647**
     Where's the information I need? Look in: *Female packaging employees in 2008 (at Pennon location)* pie chart and *Male packaging employees in 2008 (at Pennon location)* pie chart.

	Age <25	Age 25-29
Female	132	166
Male	199	150

3   **Answer (B) is correct: 286**
     Where's the information I need? Look in: *Conglomerate plc employees by function* table and *Male* and *Female packaging employees* pie charts.

Step 1: The total number of Packaging employees in 2008 is 1,622.

Step 2: Find the total number of employees at the Pennon site:
607 females + 729 males = 1,336

Step 3: Find the difference:
1,622 − 1,336 = 286 employees

4   **Answer (A) is correct: Retail**
Where's the information I need? Look in: *Conglomerate plc employees by function 2006–2008* table.
Work out each function's changes in staff numbers between 2006 and 2008:
Retail = 3,855 − 3,580 = 275 more employees
Logistics = 1,636 − 1,425 = 211 more employees
Packaging = 1,622 − 1,672 = 50 fewer employees
Food = 1,588 − 1,561 = 27 more employees
Leisure = 2,121 − 2,451 = 330 fewer employees
The question asks about the difference, so where there have been more or fewer employees. The second largest difference is Retail.

5   **Answer B is correct: £20,000**
Where's the information I need? Look in: *Conglomerate plc employees by function* table. This shows that the number of Retail employees in 2007 was 3,973.
Profits per employee = £79,460,000/3,973 = £20,000

Advanced data interpretation practice test 6

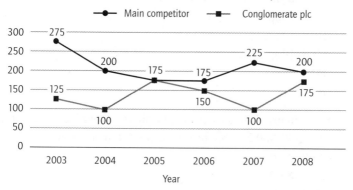

Conglomerate plc share price (pence) against main competitor

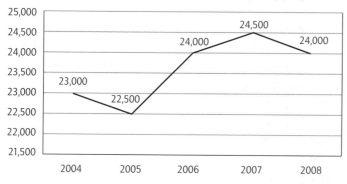

Conglomerate plc average graduate starting salary (in £)

Average UK salary by function (2008)

Function	UK industry – Average Director salary (£1,000s)	UK industry – Average graduate starting salary (£1,000s)
Engineering/IT	78.5	24.1
Operations	74.8	23.6
Marketing	75.4	22.4
Finance	89.2	23.5
Corporate	91.5	25.1

1   Over the six-year period what is the range of the price difference between the Conglomerate plc share price and its main competitor?
    (A) 0–150p
    (B) 0–125p
    (C) 0–100p
    (D) 0–75p
    (E) 0–50p

2   How many Conglomerate plc shares would a speculator with £33,000 be able to buy at the 2006 share price?
    (A) 220,000
    (B) 22,000
    (C) 2,200
    (D) 220
    (E) 22

3   If the same absolute downward trend in starting salaries between 2007 and 2008 continued between 2008 and 2009, what would the Conglomerate plc 2009 average graduate starting salary be?
    (A) £24,500
    (B) £24,000
    (C) £23,500
    (D) £23,000
    (E) £22,500

4   What is the average graduate starting salary across the five years shown?
    (A) £22,200
    (B) £23,200
    (C) £23,500
    (D) £23,600
    (E) £24,500

5   In which UK industry functions are there the greatest and the least difference between Director and graduate salaries?

(A) Corporate (greatest); Operations (least)

(B) Finance (greatest); Operations (least)

(C) Corporate (greatest); Marketing (least)

(D) Finance (greatest); Marketing (least)

(E) Engineering/IT (greatest); Operations (least)

6   What would the average Finance Director salary be in euros (to the nearest €100)? Use an exchange rate of €1.12 to the £.

(A) €93,900

(B) €95,900

(C) €97,900

(D) €99,900

(E) €101,900

Review your answers to practice test 6

1   **Answer (A) is correct: 0–150p**
Where's the information I need? Look in: *Conglomerate plc share price (pence) against main competitor* graph.
This range can be obtained by finding the largest gap between the two lines on the graph. This gives you readings of 275p compared to 125p.
$275 - 125 = 150$

2   **Answer (B) is correct: 22,000**
Where's the information I need? Look in: *Conglomerate plc share price (pence) against main competitor* graph. The average 2006 share price is £1.50.
Number of shares = 33,000/1.5 = 22,000

3   **Answer (C) is correct: £23,500**
Where's the information I need? Look in: *Conglomerate plc average graduate starting salary (2003–2008)* graph.

Step 1: Calculate the decrease in starting salary between 2007 and 2008:
£24,500 − £24,000 = £500 decrease

Step 2: Deduct this amount from the 2008 starting salary:
£24,000 − £500 = £23,500

4   **Answer (D) is correct: £23,600**
Where's the information I need? Look in: *Conglomerate plc average graduate starting salary (2003–2008)* graph.
Calculate the average:
(£23,000 + £22,500 + £24,000 + £24,500 + £24,000)/5
= £23,600

5   **Answer (A) is correct: Corporate (greatest); Operations (least)**
Where's the information I need? Look in: *Average UK salary by function (2008)* table.

Calculate the differences between Director and graduate salaries for each industry function:

Engineering/IT = 78.5 − 24.1 = 54.4

Operations = 74.8 − 23.6 = 51.2

Marketing = 75.4 − 22.4 = 53

Finance = 89.2 − 23.5 = 65.7

Corporate = 91.5 − 25.1 = 66.4

6   **Answer (D) is correct: €99,900**

Where's the information I need? Look in: *Average UK salary by function (2008)* table.

The table gives you the average Finance Director salary (£89,200). Convert this into euros:

£89,200 × €1.12 = €99,904

Advanced data interpretation practice test 7

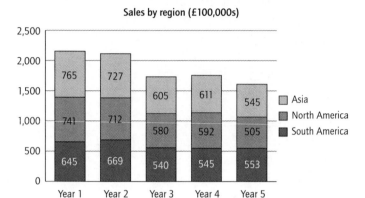

Sales by region (£100,000s)

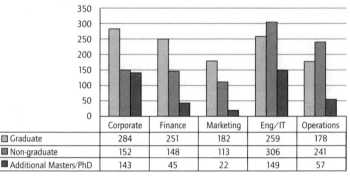

Conglomerate plc UK staff 2008 by function and qualification

	Corporate	Finance	Marketing	Eng/IT	Operations
☐ Graduate	284	251	182	259	178
☐ Non-graduate	152	148	113	306	241
☐ Additional Masters/PhD	143	45	22	149	57

1   In which year was there a greater than 10% drop in regional sales?

    (A) Year 1

    (B) Year 2

    (C) Year 3

    (D) Year 4

    (E) Year 5

2   What are the total Asian sales across Years 1–5 in euros using an exchange rate of €1.11 to the £ (to the nearest € million)?

    (A) €361 million

(B) €353 million

(C) €341 million

(D) €333 million

(E) €323 million

3   What were the total sales for North America across the five
     years in £ millions?
     (A) £313 million
     (B) £318 million
     (C) £320 million
     (D) £321 million
     (E) £323 million

4   Which function has 22.4% of the total graduate employees?
     (A) Corporate
     (B) Finance
     (C) Marketing
     (D) Engineering/IT
     (E) Operations

5   What percentage of total Engineering and IT employees are
     non-graduates?
     (A) 40%
     (B) 41%
     (C) 42%
     (D) 43%
     (E) 44%

Review your answers to practice test 7

1   **Answer (C) is correct: Year 3**
Where's the information I need? Look in: *Sales by region (£100,000s)* graph.
The graph shows that there are three possible periods when there has been a year-on-year decrease in regional sales:
Year 2 = 100% × (2,108 − 2,151)/2,151 = 2% decrease
Year 3 = 100% × (1,725 − 2,108)/2,108 = 18.2% decrease
Year 5 = 100% × (1,603 − 1,748)/1,748 = 8.3% decrease

2   **Answer (A) is correct: €361 million**
Where's the information I need? Look in: *Sales by region (£100,000s)* graph.

Step 1: Calculate the total Asian sales across all five years:
765 + 727 + 605 + 611 + 545 = 3,253

Step 2: Convert to euros:
3,253 × €1.11 = 361 (€ millions)

3   **Answer (A) is correct: £313 million**
Where's the information I need? Look in: *Sales by region (£100,000s)* graph.
Calculate the total North American earnings across all five years:
741 + 712 + 580 + 592 + 505 = 3,130 or £313 million

4   **Answer (D) is correct: Engineering/IT**
Where's the information I need? Look in: *Conglomerate plc UK staff 2008 by function and qualification* graph.

Step 1: Find the total number of graduate employees:
284 + 251 + 182 + 259 + 178 = 1,154

Step 2: Find the percentage of graduate employees within each function:
Corporate: 284/1,154 × 100% = 24.6%
Finance: 251/1,154 × 100% = 21.8%

Marketing: $182/1,154 \times 100\% = 15.8\%$
Engineering/IT: $259/1,154 \times 100\% = 22.4\%$
Operations: $178/1,154 \times 100\% = 15.4\%$
Alternatively, a much quicker calculation is to find 22.4% of $1,154 = 259$, and then see which sector has that number

5   **Answer (D) is correct: 43%**
Where's the information I need? Look in: *Conglomerate plc UK staff 2008 by function and qualification* graph.
There are 306 non-graduates working in Conglomerate's Engineering and IT functions.

Step 1: Find the total Engineering and IT employees:
$259 + 306 + 149 = 714$

Step 2: Find the percentage that are non-graduates:
$306/714 = 43\%$ (to the nearest whole per cent)

What did you think of this book?

We're really keen to hear from you about this book, so that we can make our publishing even better.

Please log on to the following website and leave us your feedback.

It will only take a few minutes and your thoughts are invaluable to us.

www.pearsoned.co.uk/bookfeedback